The

Tumblety-Lyons
Connection

J. H. Tyson

THE TUMBLETY-LYONS CONNECTION

J. H. Tyson

ISBN (Print Edition): 978-1-66783-132-9

ISBN (eBook Edition): 978-1-66783-133-6

TABLE OF CONTENTS

INTRODUCTION

"The very curious fact about Tumblety is that he is two totally different men; that is, he has lived two ... distinct lives, and there are two irreconcilable histories given of him, each by witnesses who are positive they are correct."

Bucks County Gazette, Bristol, PA, December 13, 1888

"Dr." Francis Tumblety's public persona, as expressed in his self-serving autobiography and advertisements, differed markedly from police files, negative newspaper articles, and court records. This book endeavors to sift through masses of contradictory evidence in order to present an accurate representation of his character and life experiences.

Tumblety first came to my attention while surfing through www.casebook.org, a Jack the Ripper website. Curiosity about him led me to well-researched biographies written by Timothy Riordan and Michael Hawley. Both portrayed Francis as an interesting figure in his own right, irrespective of any involvement the Whitechapel murders.

This work started out as one chapter in a longer book, tentatively titled The Fine Line, meaning the thin partition between genius and madness. However it grew out of control, burgeoning from the planned 5,000 words to 46,000. Rather than use this piece as the longest chapter ever, I decided just to make it my shortest book.

Like all of us, Francis Tumblety was born with abilities and shortcomings. He led a double life because of a split personality, and inner conflicts arising from deep-seated neuroses. Francis enjoyed good relationships with his mother and siblings, yet hated attractive young women whom he viewed as sirens luring men to doom. He posed as an eminent citizen, while selling dubious medicines and indulging in pederasty. At the same time he nominally practiced Roman Catholicism, and generously donated to charities.

Since two excellent biographies of Tumblety have already been published, a prospective reader might ask: "What fresh material does your book contain?" After rattling off today's stock interviewee response, "That's a great question," I'd respond by mentioning the following examples. It's not generally known that 15 year old Francis spent a few unhappy weeks as a merchant seaman cadet on the vessel "Success" during the summer of 1845. ... When 28 year old Isaac Golladay suddenly vanished from Washington, DC in May, 1888, police suspected his 58 year old mentor, Dr. Francis Tumblety, of foul play. That impression was reinforced when Tumblety sailed for England immediately after Golladay's disappearance. However, it turned out that Isaac, the nephew of two southern congressmen, simply returned to his hometown of Lebanon, Tennessee, where he was given a plot of land and quickly married off to a local girl. The 1930 census showed him still living in Tennessee as a 71 year old widower.

After googling the name Sophia Lyons, Tumblety's enemy and mother of his protégé George Lyons, I discovered that she was one of America's more infamous female criminals between 1870 and 1912—perhaps second only to her associate Frederika "Marm" Mandelbaum, Manhattan's premier dealer in stolen goods. That synchronicity (meaningful coincidence) revealed the fateful link between Sophie Lyons and Francis Tumblety. Those two antagonists were both immigrants, frequently in trouble with the law, who wrote books, became wealthy, and had their wills contested. My faith in karma, fate, synchronicities, (and other real phenomena that skeptics mock) increased as their intertwined stories unfolded.

A fellow writer once criticized me for "flying off point" too often. While one should stick to the topic, I find the task of entertaining (as well as informing and shocking) readers sometimes requires me to go off on tangents. In my case that tendency arises from stepping back and allowing the living composition to drift in an unanticipated direction. That's why Sophie Lyons took over chapters 3 and 9 of this work about Francis Tumblety. Other digressions would be my thumbnail sketch of "Marm" Mandelbaum, and brief dissertation on the decline of Detroit, Sophie's adopted city. Those departures from the main subject divulged things I learned in the course of writing this book, so I'm not inclined to chuck them onto the cutting room floor.

My Jack the Ripper chapter looks like a non-sequitur, but it actually bolsters this work's thesis by incriminating a much more likely suspect than Tumblety. I'm convinced Francis had nothing to do with the Ripper slayings, but he very well might have written the anonymous "From Hell Letter" to deride his perennial antagonists on London's Metropolitan Police force. A suspicious character fitting his description, inquired in a Whitechapel shop about letter recipient George Lusk's address on the same date that disturbing note was mailed. Graphologists have pointed out strong similarities between Tumblety's handwriting and that of the "From Hell Letter's" writer.

Despite his lack of education, Tumblety was very intelligent. His books—the autobiography (in several editions) and Kidnapping of Dr. Tumblety—still read well today. Sections of them were ghostwritten, even plagiarized. However, many passages written in his distinctive style demonstrate the narrative talents of an Irish bard.

Although essentially an outsider, Tumblety cultivated the persona of a prosperous social climber in his younger days. He cared about appearances and used advertising and public relations to buoy his reputation. At the same time he adopted the lifestyle of a grifter with his patent medicine huckstering, and aversion to staying long in any one place.

Inveterate newspaper reader Francis regarded the celebrities of his day as palpably real, almost as friends. He found them far more interesting than the run of humanity, and longed to be one of them. Today we would describe him as "star-struck." Endowed with boldness, Hibernian eloquence, and an uncanny ability to mimic his "betters," he often succeeded in charming the rich and famous of his time.

Though his morals left something to be desired, Tumblety's life was a classic American success story. In the late 19th Century he personified the 21st Century maxim, "fake it till you make it." It required shrewdness and determination for an immigrant born into dire poverty to master polite society's language, the pharmaceutical trade, and bond market. Enthusiastic theatergoer Francis's innate acting ability served him well. His rise from shanty Irish indigence to affluence demonstrated genuine entrepreneurial ability. By the time of his death on May 28, 1903 he'd amassed an estate valued at almost $140,000., the equivalent of $4,300,000. in year-2021 dollars.

J. H. Tyson

Media, PA

February, 2022

CHAPTER 1

The Notorious Dr. Francis Tumblety

Ireland has produced more than its share of flawed prodigies. Francis Tumblety's botched rags-to-riches story reveals a man with driving ambition, high intelligence, and charisma who could not control dark impulses.

The youngest of eleven children, Tumblety was born in 1830 near today's village of Bailieborough, on the border of counties Meath and Cavan, to parents Margaret (Nulty) Tumuelty and James Tumuelty, who worked as migrant farm laborers. (Their children used such variant surname spellings as "Tumulty," "Tumelty," and "Tumilty." Francis added the "b" to his last name for unknown reasons.)

Tumblety's older siblings were: Alice (born circa 1808, married name Fitzsimmons), Bridget aka "Biddy," (1810, Brodigan,) Julia (1812, Moore), Elizabeth aka "Betsy" (1814, Powderly), Mary (1816, Kelly), Lawrence aka "Larry" (1818), James Patrick aka "Pat" (1820), Margaret (1824, Kavanagh), Ann (1827, Mahoney), and Jane (c. 1828, Hayes.)

The family regarded Francis as an "exceptional child," implying gifted, high-strung, and not quite right. Older parents, poor nutrition, and the likelihood of an alcoholic father would account for some of his quirks. Many people in northeast Ireland were both inbred and malnourished. A high alcoholism rate prevailed among inhabitants. It would be miraculous if father James Tumuelty, a beaten down 49 year old Irish serf in the year of Francis' birth, did not drink. Tumblety biographer Michael Hawley has suggested that Margaret, like many housewives in County Meath, helped save her large brood from starvation by spinning flax into lace. I suspect that older sisters Betsy, Mary, and Margaret helped raise Francis.

A September 1845 muster roll of British Commercial Navy (Merchant Marine) inductees showed Francis as a 15 year old recruit on the vessel "Success," indentured to ship owner J. Thompson for five years. He quickly washed out of that seaman apprentice program. Francis always liked smart uniforms—and young sailors—but wouldn't have enjoyed swabbing decks, stowing cargo, or braving storms at sea. Did he receive an unfitness discharge because of his sexual orientation? If so, there's no record of it.

We next find him on the passenger list of "coffin ship" Ashburton, which sailed out of Liverpool with 330 souls aboard on May 21, 1847. Accompanying Francis were his brother Pat (29), mother Margaret (52), and sister Ann (20). They arrived in New York harbor on June 21st and settled in Rochester, where older siblings Alice Fitzsimmons, Mary Kavanagh, and Lawrence Tumelty had emigrated a few years earlier. The U. S. census recorded the family in Rochester's 8th Ward as follows on September 18, 1850: Margaret Tumathy (sic) 62, at home, Lawrence 20, gardener, Ann 22, and Francis 19, laborer, all born in Ireland. Francis then worked in an iron foundry, a job he must have hated.

A few months later he entered the medical field as an employee of Dr. Ezra Reynolds, also known as Dr. W. C. Lispenard, who operated a small clinic specializing in "French cures" for venereal diseases. In the 1850 Rochester City Directory Reynolds' full page ad proclaimed:

> This is the only office in the city where a permanent cure
> of private diseases can be had without the use of mercury
> or change of diet. We guarantee to cure gonorrhea, gleet,
> syphilis, impotency, nocturnal emissions, ... self-abuse,

diurnal emissions, female complaints, in short, every possible form of sexual disease...[1]

Certain botanicals might relieve symptoms of syphilis, but they could not cure it. Because of the embarrassment associated with sexually transmitted diseases, Reynolds could feel secure that disgruntled patients wouldn't publicly complain about his inability to clear up their "crabs" or "clap."

Francis hawked Reynolds' 224 page book, Dr. Lispenard's Practical and Private Medical Guide in Plain English, along the Erie Canal system between Rochester and Buffalo. Because this pamphlet discussed sexual aberrations and diseases, canal boat captain W. C. Streeter and other respectable citizens, deemed it pornographic.

By 1853 Francis became the assistant of traveling "snake oil" medicine man Rudolf Lyons, who touted herbal nostrums. Lyons advertised heavily, billing himself as an Indian root doctor. Though born in Maryland, he claimed South America as his birthplace because of that region's plethora of exotic plants with healing properties. Through him Tumblety became acquainted with the ideas of New Hampshire herbalist Samuel Thomson, who preached the merits of vegetable remedies, while condemning surgery, bloodletting, and toxic minerals such as arsenic, mercury, and antimony.

Both Reynolds and Lyons boasted about having psychic ability, which enabled them to diagnose patients without examining them. Lyons' Rochester City Directory ad stated: "Dr. Lyons professes to discern diseases by the eye. He therefore asks no questions, nor does he require patients to explain symptoms ...."[2] Tumblety also claimed to be endowed with second sight, which rendered both physicals and patient input unnecessary.

Young "Frank," as he was then known, did not make a favorable impression on Rochester's upper class. In December 1888 Rochester socialite and State Department official Edward Haywood told a reporter:

> I remember (Tumblety) very well, when he used to run about the canal, (as) a dirty, awkward, ignorant, uncared for, good-for-nothing boy … utterly devoid of education. He lived with his brother (Lawrence) who was my uncle's (Dr. William Fitzhugh's) gardener … The only training he ever had for the medical profession was in a little drug store at the back of … Arcade Gallery, which was kept by a 'Dr.' Lispenard, who carried on a medical business of a disreputable kind.[3]

Haywood declared that Tumblety "had no associates … when a boy, and when he returned he was more exclusive and solitary than ever."[4]

Despite his ability to imitate the superficial sociability of fellow hucksters, Tumblety was a loner. He trusted family members and a few "confidential valets," but had virtually no long-term friendships. St. Louis hotel proprietor Philo Smith and Fifth Ave. Hotel desk clerk William H. Carr, both of whom knew Francis for years, spoke of his private nature. Smith declared under oath that "no one ever got close to him."[5]

Yet from his late teens to mid-fifties Francis had an upbeat personality and sufficient communication skills to run a business that required salesmanship. The extended title of his autobiography was: "A Sketch of the Life of the Gifted, Eccentric, and World-famed Dr. Francis Tumblety, presenting an outline of his wonderful career, professional successes, and personal intimacies with renowned personages of two hemispheres."

Tumblety possessed an innate aptitude for public relations. He not only paid thousands for newspaper ads, but cultivated editors and reporters in multiple cities, showing up with gifts of candy, cigars, medicines, and liquor for journalists willing to put in a good word for him.

Francis led two compartmentalized lives: the public one as well-heeled patent medicine distributor, and secret life as a homosexual. He utilized P.R. both to pump up drug sales, and minimize reputational damage whenever he got into trouble for his "secret vices."

After gaining experience as the understudy of doctors Ezra Reynolds and Rudolph Lyons, Francis decided to sell his own line of remedies, including Dr. Morse's Indian Root Pills, Tumblety's Pimple Banisher, and Dr. Tumblety's Vegetable Compound, a laxative containing aloes, gamboges, and mandrake root. In his medical practice he specialized in skin eruptions, indigestion, constipation, and respiratory complaints, rather than sexually-transmitted disease treatments of mentors Lyons and Reynolds. But like Rudolf Lyons and Samuel Thomson, he favored plant-derived medications over "mineral poisons." (In spite of such scruples, he spiked some of his herbal potions with Perry Davis's Painkiller, a concoction of water, alcohol, opium, sugar, and who knows what else.)

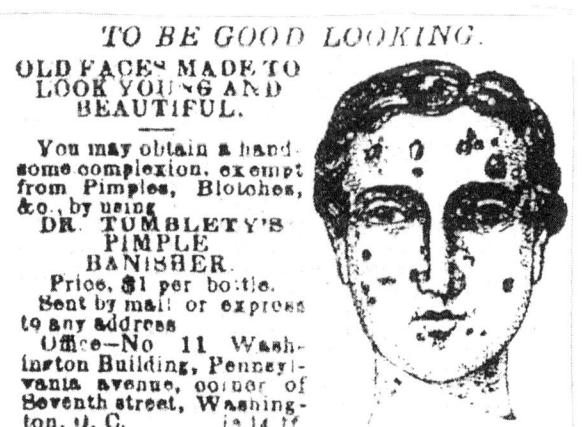

Advertisement for Tumblety's Pimple Banisher which
appeared in the Washington Evening Star, 1863

As Abraham Lincoln remarked: "You can fool some of the people all the time, and all of the people some of the time, but you can't fool all the people all the time." Tumblety could not have become a millionaire by today's standards with totally ineffectual remedies. Under the right circumstances, many of his medicines helped patients. We know that some of the testimonials he published were genuine, and others bogus. It's often difficult to distinguish between the true and false. Though most books about Francis (including this one) emphasize his charlatanry and instances of malpractice, it should be acknowledged that he did more healing than hurting. Otherwise, he would never have prospered in business for over 35 years.

Those who use aliases automatically send up the con-person red flag. Tumblety used a number of them over the years: Philip Steinburg, J. H. Blackburn, Maurice Fitzsimmons, Frank Townsend, B. R. Farrell, James Dombletree, and others. Under the name "Philip Steinburg" Tumblety opened a small shop in Rochester's Smith Block Building around 1853. Though this enterprise flourished, the restless youth realized he had to get out of Rochester to make it big. His sisters recalled a four-year absence between 1854 and 1858.

Itinerant to the point of being fly-by-night, Tumblety seemed incapable of remaining anywhere long. Compulsive travel—an earmark of what psychologists call the Narcissistic-Aggressive Personality Type—stimulated his hyperactive temperament and adventurous spirit. Dull routine in any one locale bored and depressed him. But there were other reasons for his nomadic lifestyle. As a medicine man he couldn't stay in one town indefinitely without some dissatisfied customer reporting him to local police for a bad reaction to some potion. Moreover, Tumblety not only sold questionable cure-alls, but actively engaged in homosexual activity during an era when sodomy convictions brought serious prison time. Between the

1860s and 1890s police arrested him for "unnatural offenses" in New York City, Chicago, Toronto, Cincinnati, St. Louis, New Orleans, Washington, Baltimore, London, and elsewhere. Because of his predilection for adolescent boys, he would be a registered sex offender in today's world.

Following periods in western New York State and Detroit, Tumblety moved on to Canada in 1855. Sometime during the spring of that year, he earned money hand-over-fist in London, Ontario, then decided to try his luck in Toronto. There he followed the example of Ezra Reynolds and Rudolph Lyons by publishing his first large newspaper ad with The Toronto Globe in November 1856. But this juggernaut stalled when patient Adolphus Binkert complained that Francis overcharged him for pills that made his skin eruptions worse. In the ensuing court proceeding chemist John Birks testified that Tumblety's tablets were comprised of flour, sugar, cayenne pepper, and dandelion leaf extract— ingredients very unlikely to alleviate Binkert's dermatitis. However, after Dr. Francois Alexander Hubert LaRue of Laval University confirmed that the pills did not contain any dangerous poisons, the judge threw out Binkert's case against Tumblety. However, the adverse publicity generated by this action prompted him to head for Montreal.

Over the years Francis compiled a lengthy criminal record. A Montreal detective arrested him on September 23, 1857 for selling abortion pills to 17 year old prostitute Philomene Dumas. Queasy Francis never performed an actual fetus extraction in his life, but he did prescribe abortifacients such as black hellebore. Nevertheless, he had scruples against assisting Catholic women with abortions. Ms. Dumas testified that Tumblety only agreed to hand over the tablets after being assured that she was a Protestant. Montreal Justice Gray ultimately released him for lack of evidence.

While in Montreal, Tumblety paid two hooligans to beat up comedian James B. Prior, who ridiculed his newspaper ads at a local burlesque theater. That plan backfired when Prior and his stage manager soundly thrashed the "toughs" hired by Tumblety.

In January 1859 Tumblety rented office space inside Buffalo's Concert Hall. A journalist for The Buffalo Courier who attended one of his medical lectures wrote that Francis orated with the "Thespian emphasis" of an actor.

Tumbleweed Tumblety drifted from Buffalo to Toronto sometime in late 1859. After a judge there fined him for practicing medicine without a license, he relocated to St. John, New Brunswick.

If customers were lucky, Tumblety's tonics might occasionally clear up pimples, or relieve indigestion, constipation, headache, and common cold symptoms. However, he repeatedly exposed himself to accusations of malpractice by attempting to treat critically ill people. In mid-September 1860 fifty-nine year old carpenter James Portmore and his wife Mary came to his office in St. John. Portmore had suffered from kidney and bladder stones for ten years. Tumblety sold him a bottle of transparent liquid and box of pills. After taking a spoonful or two of the syrup, Portmore's condition grew worse. He experienced severe abdominal pains. Mrs. Portmore reported Tumblety to the police, and called in her husband's former physician, Dr. Humphrey, who quickly finished off poor James with bloodletting and doses of mercury. Portmore died on September 27th. An autopsy concluded that he'd succumbed from the effects of bladder and kidney disease, with acute inflammation of the stomach noted as an aggravating factor. At the inquest chemist Mr. Barker testified that Tumblety's decoction of Irish moss, parsley, balsam copaiba, and sweet spirits of nitre might not have helped Portmore, but most likely didn't kill him. According to Tumblety biographer Timothy Riordan, balsam copaiba, a powerful diuretic derived from fir tree resin, probably caused gastric irritation. In other words, it's inadvisable to administer a turpentine-like substance to someone with sore innards.

Worried about being convicted of manslaughter, scourge-of-Canada Tumblety dashed over the U. S. border on horseback to Calais, Maine. A day or two later he arrived at sister Elizabeth Powderly's Waterloo, New York farmhouse, where he hid out for a few weeks.

At this time Tumblety loved expensive suits and jewelry. Shortly after the St. John debacle he launched an extravagant sales campaign in Boston. Attired in a Prussian Hussar uniform bedecked with medals, Francis capered about on his white horse, grasping a large bouquet of flowers in his left hand. A liveried valet followed, walking two greyhounds. Nicholas Hadley, who witnessed this spectacle, commented that he looked like "... a man in the circus ... off (his head)."[6] An expert equestrian and horse trainer, Tumblety could make his mounts trot, canter, rear up and walk on their hind legs, and do other tricks.

After attracting public notice with such ostentation, silver-tongued Tumblety would deliver impassioned speeches promoting his "miracle" drugs. Over the next six months, he used this same pitch to drum up sales in New York City, Jersey City, Philadelphia, and Baltimore.

Tumblety did not limit his fancy dress to work days. While attending Sunday mass in 1857, he "marched up the middle aisle of the principal Catholic church of Ottawa, ... preceded by his secretary carrying a large, gorgeous prayer book, ... and presented a $100. bill ($3,000. in 2021 money) as his offering."[7]

At the same time Francis aped the nouveau riche with fancy outfits, jewelry, and thoroughbred horses, he had a penchant for the wrong side of the tracks. An old acquaintance from Boston recalled him as:

A tall, fine-appearing individual. He was a most peculiar person. He wore, pinned to his vest, several large medals which he said had been awarded him in various colleges... (Yet) he liked the slums, notwithstanding the fact that he always had plenty of money, and could have entered, if he had been inclined, into good society.[8]

Between December 1860 and October 1861 Tumblety lived at The Fifth Ave. Hotel in Manhattan, and rented an office at 400 Broadway. During this period his over-the-top newspaper advertisements inspired parodies. Avid theater buff Francis clashed with Dan Bryant's Minstrels which had staged a satirical skit entitled, "Dr. Tumblety Outdone." Because of the negative publicity sparked by Bryant's performance, he began billing himself as "The Indian Herb Doctor," without using his name.

Over the years Francis employed several "confidential valets," most of whom served as both secretaries and live-in lovers. He hired Charles P. Jones in Toronto, John Guy in Montreal, and William Hamilton in St. John. Seventeen year old Charles Whelpley worked for him in New York City. One day in January 1861 Tumblety wrote out a check for one hundred dollars payable to himself, handed it to Whelpley, and instructed him to bring back the cash from Chemical Bank. A quick learner, Whelpley wrote out a check for $400. The next day he forged Tumblety's signature, pocketed the money, and absconded. Francis sued the bank for approving that unauthorized withdrawal, but lost.

Tumblety fared better with his next protégé, a 17 year old tinsmith from Brooklyn named Mark A. Blackburn, who loyally served him for the next four years.

In November 1861 Tumblety journeyed to Washington, D. C., and registered at The Willard Hotel. He lobbied Union General George

B. McClellan's staff for an appointment as surgeon to one of Army of the Potomac's 155 regiments. Colonel Charles A. Dunham remembered attending a banquet and lecture hosted by "Dr." Tumblety.

> Someone asked why he had not invited some women to his dinner. His face instantly became ... black as a thunder cloud. He had a pack of cards in his hand, but he laid them down and said almost savagely, 'No Colonel, I don't know any such cattle, and if I did I would, as your friend, sooner give you a dose of poison than take you into such danger.' He then broke into a homily on the sin and folly of dissipation, fiercely denounced all women and especially fallen women. He then invited us into his office where he illustrated his lecture ... One side of this room was entirely occupied with cases ... When the doors were opened, quite a museum was revealed—tiers of shelves with glass jars and cases ... with anatomical specimens. The "doctor" placed on a table a dozen or more jars containing the (uteri) of every class of woman ... Not long after this the "doctor" was (there) when my Lt. Colonel came in and commenced expatiating on the charms of a certain woman. In a moment (Tumblety) was lecturing him and denouncing women. When he was asked why he hated women, he said that when quite a young man he fell desperately in love with a pretty girl, rather his senior, who promised to reciprocate his affection. After a brief courtship, he married her. The honeymoon was not over when he noticed a disposition on the part of his wife to flirt with other men. He remonstrated, she kissed him, (and) called him dear jealous fool. Happening one day to pass in a cab through the worst part of town he saw his wife and a man enter a gloomy-looking house. Then he

learned that before her marriage his wife had been an inmate of that and many similar houses (of ill repute). (Thus) he gave up on all womankind.[9]

I could find no record of Tumblety ever being married. All census enumerations described him as single. It should be mentioned that he generally had good relationships with landladies, his sisters, and nieces. Approximately 30% of his patients were females.

"Colonel" Charles Dunham (a.k.a. Sanford Conover) of Fairview, New Jersey fails to qualify as a trustworthy source. At various times he operated as a lawyer, spy, yellow journalist, faux military officer, and dirty tricks specialist for the Democratic Party. In 1861 Dunham raised money to form a Union regiment, "The Cameron Guards." When that effort flopped, he allegedly converted some of its leftover funds to his own personal use, and continued wearing an officer's dress uniform all over town. Since his unit never came into existence, he didn't have to worry about being summoned to combat duty.

Dunham wrote articles under at least nine different pseudonyms for multiple newspapers. He would regularly plant a pro-Confederate story in one paper, then refute it in another publication. Dunham served time for perjury after providing false evidence to the congressional committee investigating President Lincoln's assassination. Major General John A. Dix decreed that his word must never be believed "unless corroborated by witnesses of unquestioned credibility."[10]

Despite warranted reservations about Dunham/Conover's integrity, it must be conceded that he did spend time with Tumblety, and shared keen observations concerning the machinations of a fellow scoundrel. Though we should not swallow his account whole, Tumblety undoubtedly did own "anatomical curiosities." According to an article in Vanity Fair magazine, his specimens looked "as if they might have once formed ... the collection of a lunatic confined in a leper hospital."[11] But did he exhibit them in the window of his storefront office at 400 Broadway in 1861? More sober accounts hold that his front window contained a diagram of the human circulatory system, not women's sexual organs pickled in alcohol. However, nearby dime museums did exhibit "Anatomical Venuses" which displayed female genitalia in bold relief.

Dunham's account of Tumblety's misogyny rang true. New Orleans judge Harry Patin remembered encountering him in a dark alley. "I met him in Varieties Alley and he wanted to get me in a conversation. He said men should not like women, and all those kind of things."[12] New Orleans police laboratory technician Richard S. Norris recollected Tumblety giving him a sermon on the evils of cigarettes and prostitutes.

> He said the trouble with young men are cigarettes, and those confounded street walkers. He said if he had his way they would all be disemboweled.[13]

Martin McGarry, who served as Francis's valet between 1882 and 1884, told a New York World reporter:

> Dr. Tumblety used to say to me, 'Martin, no women for me.' He always disliked women very much. He could not bear to have them near him. He thought all women were imposters, and often said that all the trouble in this world was caused by women.[14]

In his March 31, 1876 letter to Hall Caine, Tumblety revealed his contempt for Asian women.

In morals and obscenity they (Chinese females) are far below our most degraded prostitutes. Their women are bought and sold for the usual (reasons), and ... used to decoy youths of the most tender age into ... dens for the purpose of exhibiting their nude and disgusting persons to hitherto innocent (boys).[15]

Tumblety's Rejection

In early 1862 the Union Army denied Tumblety's application for a regimental surgeon's commission—perhaps owing to the small detail that he never attended medical school. (He had purchased an authentic-looking M. D. diploma from the non-existent "Eclectic Medical College of Pennsylvania," but that didn't fool General McClellan's staff.) Detective William Pinkerton affirmed that another reason for the army's rebuff was an ad campaign aimed at troops with venereal diseases. Pinkerton wrote:

He ... flooded the army with ... handbills and ... objectionable books, so much so that General McClellan issued strict orders that the circulation of (them) should be suppressed on the ground that (they) were calculated to debase the soldiers, their contents being of an immoral character and their illustrations still more so.[16]

During the Civil War Washington's population nearly doubled because of the influx of soldiers and defense contractors, fueling a boom in the bordello industry. Sensing a moneymaking opportunity, Tumblety decided to remain in the city. Newspaper ads composed by him in rhymed doggerel billed himself as the "Indian Herb Doctor."

Come and see for yourselves ye lame and suffering, Oh ye

rheumatic and dying, come and see,

Light shall again the faded eye illumine,

And rosy health the pallid cheek resume.

Thousands rescued from disease and death

Invoke God's blessings in Tumblety.

I desire your prostrate hearts to life.

Your bleeding wounds to cure,

And with the treasures of nature's gift

Relieve the rich and poor.

... No charge for Consultation or Advice.

Office #11, Washington Building, Pennsylvania Avenue, corner 7th St.[17]

Washington, D. C.'s Canterbury Music Hall produced a spoof of those misleading ads. Francis allegedly sued Canterbury's proprietor George Percival for libel. Charles Dunham thought the lawsuit story contrived, since he heard that Tumblety, an incurable ham, occasionally appeared onstage with Percival's actors in one of his ersatz uniforms. Dunham viewed him as a publicity hound who would do anything—good or bad—to attract notice.

At the same time Tumblety sullied his reputation by selling phony certificates of disability to soldiers in the New York 2nd Heavy Artillery Regiment. His flight to Frederick, Maryland in August 1862 was most likely prompted by Major Levi C. Turner's investigation into this scandal. Tumblety apparently fabricated unfitness certificates for privates Thomas Tift and George Torrey. Both men returned to duty. Private Tift died of wounds in July 1864, following the bloody Battle of Cold Harbor.

On or about May 15, 1863, Francis arrived in Philadelphia and registered at The Girard House Hotel, 9th & Chestnut streets. He signed a lease for office space at 333 Chestnut St. and placed daily advertisements in Philadelphia newspapers. Residents remembered him wearing a European cavalry uniform as he grandly rode his gray dappled horse through town.

On May 21st Tumblety reported to police that a young man named Joe St. Clair had stolen the gold medal Montreal had awarded him in 1858. Philadelphia cops quickly collared Joseph Aspinwall, alias "Joe St. Clair," who denied taking it. About a week later Tumblety withdrew his complaint, informing police that someone had slipped the purloined decoration under his office door.

In the meantime, Police Chief Benjamin Franklin telegraphed Montreal's police department and asked if that city had ever presented Dr. Francis Tumblety with a medal. After thanking Franklin for giving him a hearty laugh, either police chief Guillaume Lamothe or his adjutant responded that the city would be more inclined to provide wanted fugitive Tumblety free jail accommodations than an award for meritorious service. He then related facts about the Philomena Dumas abortion case, Francis' penchant for "unnatural vices," and his flight from St John to avoid prosecution for manslaughter in the Portmore imbroglio. Chief Franklin passed on this information to Mayor Alexander Henry, who threatened to issue a warrant for Tumblety's arrest on the charge of making a false police report if he did not leave Philadelphia by July 1st.

Francis quit the City of Brotherly Love shortly before that deadline. He first went to New York City, where he delivered inflammatory speeches for The Fenian Brotherhood during the Irish draft riots of July 1863.

Other than his Irish nationalist bent, Tumblety's political beliefs were hard to pin down. He admired Republicans Abraham Lincoln and Tom Corwin, as well as Democrats Grover Cleveland and Daniel Manning. Francis thought that the Civil War, which resulted in the deaths of 620,000

Americans, could have been avoided by means of negotiation and compromise. In the 1884 presidential election he preferred the "Rum, Romanism, and Rebellion" of Grover Cleveland to Maine's Republican Senator James G. Blaine who preached "Prohibition, Protestantism, and Prudery."

During summer of 1863 Francis also spent time in Albany, Saratoga Springs, Rochester, and elsewhere in upstate New York. Rumor placed him in the company of handsome matinee idol John Wilkes Booth while in Buffalo. According to The Buffalo Courier, "quite an intimacy sprung up between John Wilkes Booth and Dr. Tumblety."[18] The Atchison, Kansas Daily Globe wrote that Booth's friend and accomplice David Herold also had a close relationship with Francis.

(Herold) was a pale-face, large-eyed, poetical-looking boy (who) was with Tumblety constantly. He seemed a compromise between friend, companion, and servant to the doctor ..."[19]

The Brooklyn Daily Eagle stated that Herold "attached himself to the Indian Herb Doctor in the same manner in which he ... attached himself to Booth—from a womanish sort of admiration for his supposed cleverness."[20]

Those insinuations—published in December 1888—have never been confirmed. Tumblety denied ever meeting Booth or Herold. Not content to link him with that infamous pair, some papers erroneously added: "Several years later, he was an associate in New York of Charles J. Guiteau, who murdered President (James) Garfield."[21]

In December 1864 Tumblety and Mark Blackburn journeyed from Brooklyn to New Orleans, then St. Louis, where he took up residence at 50 Olive St., above an oyster saloon. Although police arrested him briefly for unauthorized wearing of a military uniform in Carondelet, he found "show me" Missourians uncharacteristically susceptible to his advertising campaigns.

Nevertheless, Tumblety's stint in St. Louis ended on a sour note. After perusing an inaccurate newspaper article, Provost Marshal Colonel J. D. Baker ordered Tumblety's arrest on May 5, 1865 for complicity in the assassination of President Abraham Lincoln. Ironically, Lincoln admirer Francis had just returned from the martyred president's funeral in Springfield, Illinois. The Missouri Democrat article Baker read originated in The New York Herald. Tumblety's former stable boy, 14 year old Thomas Pursell of Brooklyn, had snatched a lady's pocketbook containing $200. After his arrest in Brooklyn on May 2, 1865, Pursell tried to cop a plea by inventing stories about his supposed past association with actor John Wilkes Booth. He claimed to have served as Booth's errand boy in 1861, and alleged that David Herold briefly worked as Tumblety's assistant. However, Booth did not make his New York City debut until playing the lead role in Shakespeare's Richard III in March 1862. Tumblety resided in Washington D. C. during that time. Although N.Y.P.D. Superintendent John Alexander Kennedy immediately dismissed Pursell's story as "bosh," the wheels of injustice continued to grind in St. Louis.

Francis had used the alias Dr. J. H. Blackburn in St. Louis, perhaps to fit the role of father to valet Mark Blackburn, and called his business "Blackburn & Co." The federal government really wanted to detain Dr. Luke P. Blackburn, a Kentucky physician (and subsequent governor of that state) who'd been falsely accused of spreading yellow fever in the north by shipping infected clothing and bed sheets to "Yankee" cities. So Tumblety's detention appears to have been a case of mistaken identity. Days after his apprehension the feds transported Francis to Old Capitol Prison in Washington, D. C., and interrogated him. Unable to find any evidence that he conspired to murder Lincoln, they released him on May 30, 1865. Profoundly shocked by being accused of a crime he hadn't committed, Francis began writing "The Kidnapping of Dr. Tumblety, which attempted to exonerate himself and condemn the unconstitutional "star chamber" tactics employed by Secretary of War Edwin M. Stanton. Tumblety went so far as to accuse Stanton's agents of confiscating and cashing bonds he owned which were worth thousands of dollars.

To recover from the trauma of false imprisonment, Tumblety vacationed at a Saratoga Springs, New York resort where he claimed to have met generals Joseph Hooker and Ulysses S. Grant.

After visiting Cincinnati during the spring of 1866, Francis decided to open consulting rooms at 22 Longworth St. in that city. While there he published "The Kidnapping of Dr. Tumblety," which described his arrest on baseless charges of conspiring to assassinate President Lincoln.

During the summer of 1866 Tumblety's valet Mark Blackburn became infatuated with 17 year old Olivia B. Young, and eloped with her to New York City, where they were married in early October 1866. That escapade violated Tumblety's cardinal precept of resisting the wiles of young "hussies."

In Brooklyn Mark worked variously as a watchman and building materials yard employee. The marriage to Olivia Young did not work out. After their divorce Blackburn married Elizabeth Hauff in 1871. He and Elizabeth produced at least four children, one of them named "Francis" (who died at age three in 1883). Tumblety eventually made up with Mark, and willed $5,000. to him, the equivalent of $152,000. today.

Shocked by the suddenness of Blackburn's elopement, Francis relocated from Cincy to Pittsburgh that same month. He set up shop at The Fifth National Bank Building, 194 Liberty St, and did well there.

Pittsburgh citizens perceived Tumblety as a high roller, who freely gave away Cuban cigars and bottles Moet & Chandon champagne. While there he published the first edition of his autobiography.[22] In January 1868 he left Pittsburgh for Chicago, allegedly because two disgruntled female patients created a stir.

Detective William Pinkerton advised reporters that Tumblety did not last long in the Windy City.

In Chicago, along about 1869, he was detected ... indulging in the vices to which I have referred (homosexual acts) and had to fly that city ...[23]

By May 1869 newspaper ads placed Tumblety at 18 Exchange Place, Jersey City, New Jersey.

Perhaps due to his extensive criminal record, Tumblety had not become a naturalized American citizen. Hence, as a British subject, he filed a $100,000. false arrest claim against the U. S. government via the British embassy in Washington, D. C. Tumblety's letter to ambassador Sir Edward Thornton explained his position:

Honored Sir,

I am a British subject. With my father I came from Ireland to America while still a youth. I have never sought to detach myself by American naturalization from the government (into) whose jurisdiction I was born ... I was arrested, conveyed to Washington by order of Mr. Stanton, Secretary of War, thrust into the Old Capitol Prison, and incarcerated there several weeks ... I do not expect ever to regain my former condition of health. In fact, it is a measure owing to my feebleness that I have not long since made application for redress through you ... I had (applied) to your distinguished predecessor and my case was, by his agency, making favorable progress at the time of his lamentable decease...

Honored sir, your very profound obedient servant,

Francis Tumblety M.D.[24]

The British Foreign Office informed him by curt letter of May 22, 1876 that his claim had been denied. One wonders if British officials were aware of Tumblety's rap sheet in England, which included medical malpractice, "unnatural offences," and fanning the flames of Fenian anarchy.

Endnotes

1 Timothy B. Riordan, Prince of Quacks: The Notorious Life of Dr. Francis Tumblety, Charlatan and Jack the Ripper Suspect, McFarland & Co., Inc., Jefferson, NC, 2009, p. 11.

2 Ibid., p. 17, op. cit. Elyria Independent Democrat, February 25, 1863.

3 Rochester Democrat & Republican, December 3, 1888.

4 New York World, December 2, 1888.

5 Estate of Francis Tumblety Probate Proceedings, St. Louis, MO, Statement of Philo Smith.

6 Ibid, Statement of Nicholas Hadley, May 8, 1905.

7 Boston Globe, November 27, 1888.

8 Chicago Tribune, November 21, 1888.

9 Rochester Democrat & Republican, December 3, 1888.

10 Riordan, p. 94.

11 Vanity Fair, August 31, 1861.

12 Tumblety Probate Proceedings, City of St. Louis Archives, Statement of Judge Harry Patin, May 12, 1905.

13 Ibid., Statement of Richard S. Norris.

14 New York World, December 5, 1888.

15 Neil R. Storey, The Dracula Secrets, The History Press, Port Stroud, Gloucestershire, UK, 2012, p. 127, op. cit. March 31, 1876 Francis Tumblety letter to Hall Caine.

16 Chicago Daily Inter-Ocean, November 10, 1888.

17 Washington Evening Star, April 17, 1862.

18 Buffalo Courier, May 31, 1914.

19 Atchison (Kansas) Daily Globe, December 15, 1888.

20 Storey, op. cit. Brooklyn Daily Eagle, May 4, 1865.

21 New York World, December 2, 1888.

22 The seven editions of Francis Tumblety's autobiography were 1866 (Pittsburgh), 1871 (Brooklyn) 1872, (New York City), 1875 (England), 1889 (Brooklyn), 1893 (New York City), and 1900 (Baltimore).

23 Chicago Daily Inter-Ocean, November 20, 1888.

24 Francis Tumblety's April 30, 1868 letter to Sir Edward Thornton.

CHAPTER 2:
Broadened Horizons

1869 proved to be a watershed year for Tumblety. He published another edition of his autobiography, sailed back across the Atlantic for the first time since his emigration to America in 1847, and launched lucrative operations in England, which would be repeated until 1889. Francis also toured the European continent, where he claimed to have cured Emperor Napoleon III of scrofula, and simultaneously become a favorite courtier of Prussia's King Wilhelm I, soon to defeat Napoleon III, and become Emperor of united Germany.

Francis Tumblety, circa 1869, in a costume resembling the uniform of a Hussar calvary officer attached to Prussian King Wilhelm I's Imperial Guard. It first appeared in the 1871 edition of Tumblety's autobiography.

To test Britain's market for his drugs, Tumblety cruised to Liverpool on the steamer Nebraska in July, 1869. He changed his title from The Indian Herb Doctor to Great American Doctor to distinguish himself from Hindu fakirs. During that trip he visited Cork, Ireland and met Dr. Richard Barter, a hydro-therapist who hyped Turkish baths. Tumblety returned to New York City on September 13th. He earned an average of 200 pounds per day in England, or almost $4,000. in today's currency. Because business was so brisk, he sailed to England for the next nineteen years.

In March 1870 Francis rode by rail to San Francisco to visit sister Jane Hayes, who lived with her husband Daniel and son John in Vallejo. There were farms and orchards to the east of Vallejo which grew strawberries, grapes, olives, sunflowers, figs, walnuts, plums, avocadoes,...Tumblety viewed temperate California as a fertile paradise— the polar opposite of barren Ireland during the potato famine of his childhood. While there he purchased a fine Arabian horse for 15 year old nephew John Francis Hayes.

By April Tumblety moved to a suite in Frisco's classy Occidental Hotel, leased office space at 20 Montgomery St., and advertised in local papers. Francis subsequently moved his office to 30 Kearney St. where he utilized the Respirometer, a contraption designed to measure patients' breathing capacity. Tumblety's newspaper ads glorified him as a supernatural healer comparable to Jesus.

The age of miracles would seem reinstated in the wonderful doings of Dr. Tumblety of No. 30 Kearney St., whose recent visit to this city is attended by so many and such incredible cures of bed-ridden and crippled patients. It is well-known to hundreds in this community that in a short time he has totally removed the infirmities of months and years. Instances are known of his causing the limping cripple to lay down his crutches, without which locomotion was impossible ... The dumb have been enabled to talk, and the helpless invalid restored at once to health and happiness.[1]

On June 13th the 1870 census pinpointed him in a 5th Ward San Francisco boardinghouse: "Frederick (sic) Tumblety, 45, herb doctor, single, 1,000 estate, born in England." He returned to New York City in September of that year.

Francis Tumblety about 45 years old (circa 1875). This photo belongs to The Manx National Heritage Library's Hall Caine Collection. It first appeared in Neil R. Storey's book, The Dracula Secrets.

On page 5 of his 1893 autobiography Tumblety displayed an authentic-looking letter of commendation from French Military Ambulance Commandant P. Herve Du Lorin which thanked him for medical services rendered to French citizens during The Siege of Paris (September 1870 to January 1871). At the same time Francis claimed to be saving afflicted French citizens and soldiers, he bragged about his intimate friendship with German Emperor Wilhelm I, victor over France in the Franco-Prussian War. In the 1871 edition of his autobiography, he published a photo of himself attired in the uniform of a German cavalry officer, with the explanation:

His Majesty at ... first expressed a desire to consult me upon matters pertaining to the United States and our subsequent converse was as free and affable as between two equals in rank. I was honored with an appointment (to) his medical staff, and a photograph taken in Berlin ... at the instance of the king which represents me as I appeared in the uniform of the Imperial Guard.[2]

Those supposedly concurrent services to combatants Germany and France don't fit Tumblety's known time-line. He resided in San Francisco until September 1870 when he moved to 284 Fulton St. in Brooklyn. His advertisements in Brooklyn newspapers continued through August 1871.

Conman Tumblety was a gifted actor with an almost mediumistic ability for mimicry. Particularly between the ages of twenty-five and fifty, Tumblety could radiate personal charm, or an authoritative mien, as if impersonating the character in a play.

Although he sometimes seemed dandified and effeminate, Francis had sufficient audacity and an Irish temper. When provoked he'd strike back at opponents. His rap sheet included charges of battery. Tumblety allegedly booted asthmatic patient Fenton Scully down the steps of his Brooklyn office in 1864. (Justice Perry dismissed that case because Tumblety produced two witnesses who denied Scully's allegations.) At the Fifth Ave. Hotel's bar in 1872 he hit Frank Leslie's Illustrated Weekly's editor Ralston in the face with his glove and challenged him to a duel for publishing accounts of Canadian patients who'd suffered ill effects from his medications. According to The New York Sun,

Ralston preferred fists on the spot, and drubbed him. Detective Timothy Golden arrested Tumblety on the spot, but as Ralston had satisfaction, he refused to prosecute.[3]

Tragic Occurrences

The Tumulty clan suffered its share of tragedies. In 1858 Francis's 39 year old brother Patrick worked as a fireman for Rochester's gas lighting works. On September 20th of that year he tried to move the hearth of his wooden cabin into a new brick dwelling under construction with the idea of making it that home's kitchen. While so doing, the stone chimney collapsed, fracturing his skull. He died ninety minutes later.

Francis' sister Ann, the wife of Waterloo, New York shoemaker Jeremiah Mahoney passed away in 1863 at age thirty-five, leaving her husband with two sons under five.

Older sister Bridget ("Biddy") married laborer Christopher Brodigan circa 1839. They lived in the Liverpool suburb of West Derby with their three children. Unfortunately, she suffered a nervous breakdown in August 1854 and was confined to an insane asylum until January 15, 1855. Forty-six year old Bridget died on February 2, 1869.

1873 turned out to be another bad year for Tumblety. His 82 year old mother Margaret died. Then the Panic of 1873 hit, and lasted four years. Its causes were manifold: lingering post-Civil War inflation, the tanking of railroad stocks, devaluation of silver, and failure of Jay Cook's Bank, which set off a chain reaction of additional bank failures.

The resulting depression wiped out most of Tumblety's savings. After that crushing blow, Francis proved his entrepreneurial mettle by regaining millionaire status within two years.

Tumblety decided to transfer business operations to England. In July 1873 he sailed from New York to Liverpool on the Williams & Guinon vessel Idaho. After trips to London and elsewhere, he returned to Liverpool and established a practice at 177 Duke St. Along the way Tumblety acquired a new protégé, 18 year old carpenter Henry Carr. According to a December 1873 London Times article Carr became disenchanted with "the gentleman's manner,"[4] and returned to his parents' home in London with a gold chain Tumblety had given him. After he tried to hock this item at Parr's pawn shop, police arrested him. At his hearing Magistrate Mansfield acquitted Carr, but confiscated the chain, and presumably returned it to Tumblety.

In December 1874 forty-four year old Tumblety met a nervous 21 year old journalist (and future best-selling novelist) named Thomas Henry Hall Caine. Some observers perceived them as a "Mutt and Jeff" combination since Francis was over six feet tall, and Hall about 5' 2". Excerpts from Tumblety's letters betray the intensity of his feelings for Caine.

> Though I have been long silent, you have not been absent from my remembrance. The ultimate friendship which has subsisted between us for so long ... has prompted me to feel lively interest in all that concerns your welfare and happiness.[5]

By "ultimate friendship" Tumblety meant "Sophrosyne," Greek for the higher form of homoerotic love between an older man and young male. It consisted not merely of carnal love, but mutual development of body, mind, and character. According to this "Uranian" ideology, homosexual soldiers fought with conspicuous valor in battle to safeguard their beloved partners. In civilian affairs they tended to be more principled than money-grubbing householders who had materialistic wives and a gaggle of children to support.

Tumblety might have vaguely approached the Hellenic ideal of "Sophrosyne" via long term relationships with Mark Blackburn, Hall Caine, and Martin McGarry, but certainly not in his innumerable one-night stands with young blue-collar males.

The romance between Tumblety and Caine lasted—on and off—for about two years. Francis tried to persuade hypochondriac Hall to become involved in the drug business, but Caine did not want to leave his promising career as a drama critic and fiction writer to sell nostrums of doubtful efficacy.

Francis also badgered him to ghost-write an expanded version of his autobiography, but professional journalist Caine had by then brought his would-be mentor into focus as an imposter. Tumblety crowed about receiving the Legion of Honor from Emperor Napoleon III for healing his unsightly scrofula. He spoke fondly of cordial relationships with Abraham Lincoln, Horace Greeley, Dr. Oliver Wendell Holmes, and Emperor Wilhelm I of Germany. Though Hall never saw him in the company of celebrities, incurable name-dropper Tumblety insisted that he'd hobnobbed with British luminaries such as Earl Thomas De Grey, Baron George Allanson-Winn, Sir Wilfred Lawson, Frederick Stanley (16th Earl of Derby), Sir Charles Abbott (Lord Chief Justice of the King's Bench), and former Prime Minister Benjamin Disraeli.

The situation further deteriorated when Tumblety hired a less scrupulous hack to finish the upcoming edition of his semi-fictional autobiography, then insisted that Caine pay the printer's bill. In spite of this strife, another version of his autobiography, Passages from the Life of Dr. Francis Tumblety, did roll off the presses in March 1875.

Meanwhile, other problems cropped up. One of his patients, carpenter William Carroll, sued for 200 pounds when Tumblety, without authorization, made him a laughingstock by using his name in an embarrassing newspaper advert: "My face was covered with pimples and blotches and my blood was very impure. The Great American Doctor of 177 Duke St. has cured me." William Carroll, 2 George's Road, West Derby, Liverpool."[6]

On January 11, 1875 alcoholic railroad worker Edward Hanratty and his wife Ann showed up at Tumblety's Duke St. office. Though only 45 years old, Edward suffered from chest pains, abdominal distress, and chronic respiratory congestion. Tumblety sold him a bottle of foul-tasting brown syrup and box of pills for two pounds. Mrs. Hanratty administered one tablespoon of this liquid to her husband at five in the afternoon. Shortly before 9 PM she found him dead.

Ann Hanratty startled Tumblety when she and her friend Mrs. Johnstone barged into his office the next day, and demanded that he sign her husband's death certificate. He declined to do so. When Ann returned the next day, Francis refunded the two pounds she paid, but still refused to sign Edward's certificate of death. An autopsy conducted by Dr. J. Campbell Brown concluded that the decedent expired from natural causes, not poisoning. At the January 18th inquest Tumblety's lawyer, Mr. Murphy, questioned Edward Hanratty's regular physician, Dr. John Bligh, who acknowledged that his patient had a history of lung, heart, and liver ailments, complicated by alcoholism and smoking. The grand jury voted not to indict Tumblety for involuntary manslaughter on January 23rd, but reproved him for administering potent stimulants to a seriously ill patient without properly examining him.

By condemning him as a mountebank in a series of articles The Liverpool Leader ruined Tumblety's practice. In a vitriolic letter to Hall Caine, Francis cursed the Leader's owner and senior editor Richardson.

The proprietor of that filthy sheet The Leader is the Champion Black Mailer of England. He is one of the most infamous scoundrels ever vomited upon earth from the basement ... of hell ... The stench of him is an offence in the nostril(s) of all decent and cleanly people. He is worse than the Colorado potato beetle ... His little soul steeped in sin will go straight to the devil who has got a mortgage on him. He is as remorseless and cruel as a Comanche Indian. It would be a libel on ... dog(s) to call him a brute ...[7]

Because such bad press had destroyed the market for his remedies in Liverpool, Francis moved to a fashionable London apartment in the heart of the city's gay district at Glasshouse & Regent streets overlooking Piccadilly Circus. When sales continued to sag in July, Tumblety relocated to Birmingham. After that initiative foundered by September, he gave up and sailed back to New York.

Tumblety still pined for Hall Caine in the ensuing months, and wished to keep their "bro-romance" alive. On December 30th he wrote from San Francisco:

... It gives me infinite pleasure to hear from you and I should dearly love to see your sweet face and spend an entire night in your company.[8]

Since the California bond market had crashed during the fall of 1875, Francis penned notes pleading for money, which Caine disregarded, thus ending their relationship.

Hall Caine married Mary Chandler in 1886 and by her had two sons, both of whom would become members of Parliament. Publisher Gordon R. H. Caine represented East Dorset as a Tory from 1922 to 1945. Actor

Derwent Hall Caine served as Labour M.P. for Everton between 1929 and 1931. Despite unconfirmed rumors that Hall carried on a homosexual relationship with his friend Bram Stoker, he and Mary Chandler Caine remained married until his death on August 31, 1931.

Remembering Tumblety's pitiful condition in November 1875, New York City court stenographer Clement Bennett told a newspaper reporter in December 1888: "The last time I saw (him) he was looking shabby, careworn, lame. He appeared to be living a dissolute ... life, and was begging for a night's lodging."[9]

Tumblety managed to work his way out of that slump. By October, 1877, after trips to San Francisco and St. Louis, resilient Francis carried a thick wad of bills in his money belt, and moved into Manhattan's five star Northern Hotel on Cortlandt St.

Endnotes

1 San Francisco Chronicle, April 7, 1870.

2 Michael L. Hawley, Jack the Ripper Suspect Dr. Francis Tumblety, Sunbury Press, Mechanicsburg, PA, 2018, pp. 78-79.

3 New York Sun, November 19, 1888.

4 Times of London, December 1, 1873.

5 Francis Tumblety's May 15, 1875 letter to Hall Caine.

6 Timothy Riordan, Prince of Quacks, McFarland & Co., Jefferson. NC, 2009, p. 146, quoting Tumblety's advertisement in the November 2, 1874 edition of The Liverpool Mercury.

7 Neil R. Storey, The Dracula Secrets, The History Press, Stroud, Gloucestershire, 2012, pp.123-124, op. cit. Francis Tumblety's August 14, 1875 letter to Hall Caine. While doing research for his book The Dracula Secrets, Neil Storey discovered more than fifty of Tumblety's letters to Caine in The Manx National Heritage library at Douglas, Isle of Man. Hall's father, blacksmith John Caine, had been born and raised on a Manx farm, but emigrated to Liverpool for economic reasons in the early 1850s. As a boy Hall regularly visited his beloved (and apparently psychic) grandmother Isabella Caine in the village of Ballavolley. Owing to his attachment to her and the Isle, Caine willed his private papers to the Manx National Heritage organization sometime before his death in August, 1931.

8 Ibid., p. 126, op. cit. Francis Tumblety December 30, 1875 letter to Hall Caine.

9 San Francisco Examiner, November 27, 1888.

CHAPTER 3:

The Lyons Affair

While strolling along Lower Manhattan's Battery Park during the autumn of 1877, a forlorn-looking 11 year old boy named George Edward Lyons (born in Massachusetts on July 18, 1866) caught Francis Tumblety's eye. He struck up a conversation with the lad, and listened to his sad tale. According to George, his parents were criminals who'd abandoned him. Francis promised to help him out. We're left guessing about his true intentions. Was that humanitarian Tumblety speaking, who had a soft spot for needy children, or the calculating seducer of young males?

In spring of that year Tumblety decided to take a long vacation in Europe. To keep George afloat during his absence, he gave him $7,000. worth of South Carolina railroad bonds, so the youth could use dividends from them for spending money.

Health concerns played a role in Tumblety's decision to go abroad. He'd apparently become ill with venereal disease, which manifested as aching joints, skin eruptions, low-grade fever, runny nose, and chills. For the rest of his life he would spend weeks at spas such as White Sulphur Springs, West Virginia, Hot Springs, Arkansas, and Saratoga Springs, New York. Tumblety used cosmetic powder to cover unsightly blemishes on his face. The New York World found it ironic that one of his best-selling products had been a pimple cream, which obviously did not work on himself.

> For twenty years he has been widely known as the manufacturer of Tumblety's Pimple Banisher ... His own face is covered with pimples, and although his features are

otherwise regular, his appearance on this account is somewhat repulsive.[1]

From April 23rd to May 12th, 1878 Tumblety crossed the Atlantic aboard the steamship Montana. During that trip Francis visited numerous European capitals, including Rome, where he met Pope Leo XIII. He did not return home until April 1880. During his period abroad Francis wrote several didactic letters to "surrogate son" George Lyons.

When he arrived back in New York City, his young protégé could not be found. Tumblety soon discovered that the bonds had been cashed in for their full $7,000. face value. It turned out that George was the son of notorious thief Sophia Van Elkan Lyons (1847-1924), who'd racked up more than fifty arrests during her illicit career. She operated as a pickpocket, confidence woman, extortionist, shoplifter, bank robbery participant, jewelry thief, and favorite of Frederika "Marm" Mandelbaum, New York City's foremost dealer in stolen goods.

Sophie was born in Lauben, Bavaria on December 24, 1847 to Jewish "embroiderer" Jacob Marcus Van Elkan (1820-1895) and either Rachel Levy, or Frederika Maria Levy. She claimed that "stepmother" Frederika—who went by "Mary" in the U. S.—had turned her into a pickpocket and shoplifter by age six. Although Sophie despised her, Mary very well might have been her biological mother. Whether mother or stepmother, Frederika Maria Levy Van Elkan served numerous jail terms, including three long stretches for larceny in Sing Sing between 1867 and 1879. According to Sophie, Mary inculcated criminality by rewarding her for stealing, and meting out punishment if she came home empty-handed. Mary's regime of discipline supposedly consisted of severe beatings and torture inflicted with red-hot iron pokers.

Eight year old Sophie, sister Caroline (14), and brothers Simon (11), Gerhardt (10) and Marcus (3) arrived in New York City aboard the ship Von Stein on December 26, 1855. Jacob Van Elkan, who then worked as a pushcart peddler in Manhattan, had emigrated a year earlier. He and his family lived in a crowded tenement at 48 Columbia St. on the Lower East Side area known as "Little Germany." Ambitious Jacob soon opened his own store. The 1860 U. S. census recorded the family as Jacob Alken (sic) 40, clothing store, Mary 41 (born in Bremen), Caroline 19, Simon 17, George 15, Sophia 13, Myer 11, Mary 6, and Sarah 4 months.

Unsurprisingly, the 1860 U. S. census also enumerated 12 year old Sophia Van Elkan in the Girls Reformatory on Randall's Island. Though not a fan of America's penal system, she gave it credit for teaching her how to read, write, and render professional-grade nursing care.

In 1896 Sophie granted an interview with a New York World reporter in which she condemned both of her parents. However, she subsequently put all of the blame on her mother, implausibly claiming that father Jacob didn't know anything about her pickpocketing and shoplifting. In fact, many Lower East Side neighbors considered Jake a "ganef" and referred to him as "Elkan the Fence." In 1859 police arrested him for perjury. In 1862 he received an 18 month prison term for trying to frame a competitor on false charges of theft.

Possibly seeking a father image, Sophie married four felons: pickpocket Morrie Harris when she was 15 (circa 1863), bank burglar Ned Lyons (1865), bank robber "Big Jim" Brady (1888), and sneak thief Billy Burke (1910). She never properly split from Morrie Harris. Since her divorce from Ned Lyons for battery and desertion didn't become effective until 1892, the marriage to Jim Brady on December 11, 1888 was bigamous. Sophie evidently found Irishmen attractive, since three of her four husbands were Irish. That had the unintended consequence of making at least five of her seven children half-Irish, which might explain why their behavior so often puzzled and annoyed her.

Bank "cracksman" Ned Lyons (1839-1907) also operated as a bounty jumper during the Civil War. He claimed to have joined the Union Army multiple times, collected a $300. enlistment bounty on each occasion, then deserted. ($300. then would be equivalent to $65,000. today.)

Sophie described Ned Lyons as "a desperate scoundrel ... (who) could not leave drink alone."[2] He was also a habitual gambler and brawler. In one bar fight Philadelphia hooligan Jimmy Haggerty bit half of his left ear off. The deformity of that injury bothered Ned less than worry about being more noticeable to cops.

To garner his own $300. bounty Sophie's father Jacob took a cue from Sophie's crooked fiancé Ned, and joined one of New Jersey's volunteer infantry regiments on April 5, 1865, four days before the war officially ended. One would be justified in suspecting that 45 year old "Elkan the Fence" paid a kickback to the Tammany Hall stooge who arranged that unwarranted enlistment bonus after all fighting had ceased. Three months later the army discharged him from his inactive unit.

In 1890 Jake had the effrontery to apply for a disability pension, even though his 12 week hitch consisted exclusively of drilling and gold-bricking—supplemented by selling contraband to his much younger camp mates, who no doubt dubbed him "Old Timer," "Pop," or "Gramps." Elkan claimed that his "rheumatism, dyspepsia, ... diseases of the lungs, liver and kidneys"[3] were all service-related. Though the physician who examined him attributed those maladies to "vicious habits and old age,"[4] government bureaucrats in the War Department granted Elkan a pension of $6. per month (about $182. in 2021), and subsequently bumped it up to $12. ($364.).

After her father's death on September 1, 1895, Sophie paid the Pratt Grand Army of the Republic Post in Kingston, New York to adorn his grave at Wiltwyck Cemetery with a brass Civil War veteran's marker, plus small American flag on Decoration Day. She knew that, despite the dodgy circumstances of his military service, Elkan loved America and wanted to be remembered as a patriot. Like her, he had a good side. When counting her blessings, Sophie appreciated that the old man hadn't abandoned his children, but brought them to the U. S., where Jews could advance beyond second-class citizenship. Elkan made sporadic efforts to protect and support her as a child. After an unproductive thieving expedition as an eleven year old, one can imagine Sophie coming to his store, and getting enough cash from him to appease her rapacious mother.

Scandalous Adulthood

> "Thou shalt not steal."
> Exodus 20:15

A New York detective once stated that Sophie had a "yard" of aliases, including Sophie Elkins, Kate Wilson, Madame DeVarney, Mary Watson, Kate Lucas, plus various combinations of her middle name (Sarah), mother's maiden name (Levy), and married last names (Harris, Lyons, Brady, Burke).

Sophie flouted conventional morality by subscribing to a hedonistic, quasi-Freudian "moral" code which held that it was unnatural and injurious to resist amorous "affinities." In her mind that glib rationalization vindicated her affairs with unsavory characters such as burglar "Dutch Fred" Bennett, horse-racing tout and bookie Hamilton "Ham" Brock, and fellow thief Edward "Tammany" Mason. Sophie and bank sneak Billy Burke were lovers years before they tied the knot in Canada on February 12, 1910.

Handsome "Billy the Kid" Burke had been an enthusiastic womanizer since adolescence. When Detroit Free Press reporter Bertha O'Brien brought up his infidelities to Sophie in an interview, she replied:

> Billy Burke is ... a great man. None of your little weaklings afraid of (their) own shadow. He's the kind of (guy) who does things ... Most men never do anything—they just ... blab a lot ... Why shouldn't I love him and be loyal to him? True, he loves pretty women and every new one he sees, he's after. But what of that? Isn't that perfectly natural? And I love him for it.[5]

Sophie delivered at least seven children: George Lyons (born 1866), Florence Lyons (1868), Eugenia Lyons (1869, who died in an orphanage), Victor (aka Carleton C. Mason, 1874), Mable (1876, who died of scarlet fever in a Catholic convent school), Lottie (1878), and Sophia Madeline Brady (1891). Depending upon her mood swings, Sophie by turns loved, abused, and neglected her children.[6] She sent all of them to boarding schools, and explained her long absences to principals by claiming to be an actress on tour. As her abandoned daughters grew up, Sophie became estranged from them. During those periods she only remained on good terms with son Victor, who managed to stay far away from her while in the Navy, Massachusetts, and Washington State.

Sophie Lyons' New York City mug shot, 1886, later published in *Professional Criminals of America* by Police Chief Thomas F. Byrnes. The "witch hat" she's wearing contained a veil under its brim which could be pulled down to hide her face.

In 1886 New York City police chief Thomas F. Byrnes published Professional Criminals of America, which contained a brief profile of Sophie. It described her as 5' 2" tall, 115 pounds, ethnically Jewish, married, and the mother of four (sic) children. Byrnes characterized her as a "shoplifter, pickpocket, and blackmailer."[7] (Others also accused her of being a "pennyweight," or thief who substituted worthless pieces of costume jewelry for valuable items.) Besides several six month terms on Blackwell's Island for picking pockets and retail theft, Sophie did hard time for more serious crimes such as bank robberies. New York City police arrested her for grand larceny on October 9, 1871, which led to a five year sentence at Sing-Sing Correctional Facility. With aid from husband Ned Lyons, Sophie escaped on December 19, 1872, and fled to Montreal. Four years later, on October 26, 1876, police recaptured her on Long Island, trying to pick pockets at the Suffolk County Fair, and sent her back to Sing-Sing. Chief Byrnes concluded his unflattering outline of her career by adding an untrue accusation: "Of late she has become addicted to opium."[8]

Sophie did not simply rot in Sing Sing. She learned first aid and licensed practical nursing. After her release in fall of 1877 Sophie discovered to her chagrin that husband Ned Lyons had taught their son George the rudiments of burglary and safe-cracking.

At this juncture she decided to divide her time between Detroit and New York City, with the long-term goal of relocating permanently to Detroit. Heat from the N.Y.P.D. had grown too intense. Detroit was just a ferry ride from Canada, which then had no extradition treaty with the U. S. But things did not go swimmingly at first. After being arrested for shoplifting in December, 1877 Sophie experienced a meltdown in Detroit House of Correction, and tried to hang herself. By the spring of 1878 she pulled herself together, and decided to reunite in Boston with former partner in crime "Red Kate" Leary.

Police Chief Thomas Byrnes wrote that Sophie "blackmailed scores of businessmen throughout the country,"[9] while posing as a prostitute. In league with Kate Leary, she lured Boston attorney Charles W. Allen into her hotel room on July 9, 1878, then shook him down for $10,000. hush money. After handing her a check for that amount, which bounced, he contacted police. In an effort to defuse this scandal, Allen declined to press charges against Lyons and Leary. However, Boston Globe police reporters picked up this story, which torpedoed his law practice.

The Rebellious Son

A flare-up between 13 year old George Lyons and his mother made news in early 1880, while Francis Tumblety still toured Europe. On January 31st Sophie brought her son into Essex Market Police Court in Manhattan and demanded that he be confined to a juvenile detention facility for chronic misbehavior, which included running away from home, truancy, deliberate disobedience, verbal abuse toward herself, and his "caretaker" Kate Woodward, whom he recently threatened with a knife. The New York Times described Sophie as "stylishly dressed," while George was "clothed in rags."[10] To Police Magistrate William Murray she declared:

> I found him yesterday in the street and I have learned that
> he has been going around drinking in saloons and singing. I
> have sent him to three different schools, but I could not keep
> him in any of them, and now I want him sent to The House
> of Refuge.[11]

Magistrate Murray asked George what he had to say for himself. He replied:

> May I tell you the whole truth? ... That woman is the wife of
> Edward Lyons, the burglar. Ask the detectives who he is and
> who she is. ... She herself is a thief ...[12]

Engraving of Sophie Lyons, circa 1889, from Joseph C. Grannan's
Pocket Gallery of Noted Criminals, Grannan Detective Bureau
Co., Warner & Heil Printers, Cincinnati, Ohio, 1890.

With that Sophie, "pale with anger, sprang toward him and struck him a hard blow in the face."[13] The truth hurt. Police officers intervened, and Justice Murray ordered them to escort her out of the courtroom.

The New York Times provided a different version of events. According to the Times article George interrupted his mother's statement before Justice Murray by shouting: "That woman is a thief and shoplifter. I have seen her steal in Montreal and elsewhere!"[14] He accused Sophie of being a loose woman who neglected him. "Yes, you want to get rid of me, and you're my mother. How can I tell you are when you have two husbands with whom you go all over the country, stealing everywhere?"[15]

After Sophie's removal from the courtroom George related how his parents, when not imprisoned, traveled incessantly, using various "crash pads" as hideouts where they stored booty and planned crimes with confederates. When out of town his mother palmed George off on Mrs. Woodward, a suspected fence who managed a secondhand goods store on Ninth Ave.

> I remained there about five months, and got 25 cents a week, my board, and some dirty old clothes. Then I went away and took a bed at The Boys Lodging House in West Thirty-fifth St. and began peddling flowers for a florist. He made me work from 6 o'clock at night until 8 or 9 the next morning. While selling flowers in the saloons I met Dan Kerrigan. He heard that I had a good voice, and ... engaged me to sing. A man who had seen me at Kerrigan's told me he would give me a home. ... I met my mother on Ninth Ave. yesterday for the first time in many months ...[16]

After returning to the courtroom subdued Sophie admitted brushes with law enforcement, but insisted she diligently tried to prevent her children from becoming delinquents. Daughters Florence and Lottie had been educated at convent schools in Canada. She reiterated her account of enrolling George in three different boarding schools, implying that he'd been expelled from all of them.

Justice Murray ordered George held in custody until contradictory allegations from both sides could be resolved through investigation. According to The New York Times, when George heard this he cursed, struggled against bailiffs, cried, then tried to choke himself by swallowing a handkerchief.

A New York Herald story claimed that the suicide attempt occurred later, while he was confined to a juvenile detention facility. "He shouted, kicked, and screamed, 'I want to go to my mother!' Warden Daly found him in the act of hanging himself."[17]

Worried about George's welfare, Sophie dropped her request to have him committed. At his release hearing a few days later Justice Murray asked him to sing a song for those present. He sung "Ave Maria" so beautifully that it brought nearly everyone to tears. Alderman Thomas Sheils offered to place him in a good foster home. Justice Murray encouraged him to visit his friend Father Edward McGlynn, a noted Catholic youth counselor and social reformer.

Despite all the melodrama and good wishes, no happy Hollywood ending transpired for George Lyons. On June 8, 1880 the U. S. census recorded him incarcerated at the House of Refuge, a grim juvenile detention center located on Randall's Island.

Tumblety vs. Lyons and Lyons vs. Tumblety

Possibly unaware of her infamy, Francis Tumblety decided to sue Sophia Lyons. During a deposition hearing on July 1, 1880 his ire rose when Sophie's attorney William P. Burr, Esq. asked the irrelevant but leading question: "What (medical) institution had the honor of graduating so precious a pupil?"[18] If Francis answered Eclectic Medical College of Pennsylvania—the defunct institution on his office diploma—he would have committed perjury. Lawyer James McClelland saved him by raising an objection, which Judge Charles Donahue sustained.

Burr further incensed Tumblety by introducing into evidence a Police Gazette article dating back to 1861 which pilloried him as a charlatan. He also knew about Tumblety's lengthy police record for homosexual activity.

In an effort to fend off his larceny allegations, 13 year old George Lyons, at the prompting of his mother, reported Francis Tumblety to police for "atrocious assault." Undeterred, Francis pressed forward his case against Sophia Lyons, whom he suspected of masterminding the $7,000. theft ($190,000. in today's money.)

It's not an established fact that Francis Tumblety sexually abused George Lyons. Most of Tumblety's male partners—Mark Blackburn, Matthew McGarry, Hall Caine, Richard Norris, etc.—were between 17 and 28. George Lyons, who was only eleven in early 1878, might have been too young for the "doctor." Then again, maybe not. Years later attorney Robert H. Simpson testified that 70 year old Tumblety molested a prepubescent boy in 1900 at Baltimore's Druid Hill Park.

> He had met him on the street and talked to him and bought him some candy, ... took him out to the park, ... and it seems

as if the little boy went home and told his mother some story, (and) where Tumblety could be found.[19]

Simpson went on to say the boy's mother, who lived near the park on Pierce St., reported Tumblety to police. To make this problem go away Francis took Simpson's legal advice and paid her $100. ($3,300. in 2021 dollars) not to press charges.

Sophie Lyons disapproved of her unruly son's relationship with Tumblety, and had no compunction about cashing in the bonds he'd so foolishly left with an eleven year old kid. As a professional extortionist she didn't shrink from employing blackmail to avoid prosecution and retain the bond proceeds.

In spite of Mrs. Lyons' palpable guilt, Judge Donahue dismissed this case on a technicality. Sophie had been savvy enough to have son George convert the bonds to cash at the office of securities brokers Boardman & Boardman. Thus, she did not personally commit larceny.

William Burr recalled this case eight years later, when Tumblety came under suspicion for the Ripper murders.

(In 1880) he brought a suit against Mrs. Lyons, charging her with the larceny of $7,000. Worth of bonds and I was retained to defend her. It seems that ... years before he met the son of Mrs. Lyons while walking on the Battery. The lad had just come from (school) and was a fine-looking young man. He was out of employment. Tumblety greeted him and soon had him under complete control. He made him a sort of secretary in the management of his bonds ... When Tumblety got back, the young man had disappeared and the mother was arrested, charged by the 'doctor' with having taken the bonds.

I remember the examination to which I subjected him at the Tombs Police Court. ... He ... refused to answer (where he obtained his medical degree). ... I thought he would spring at me to strike. There was quite a commotion in court. The case fell through and the old lady was not held ...[20]

Francis then tried to sue Boardman & Boardman, as well as his bond broker William P. O'Connor. Those efforts failed to recoup any money. The financial instruments in question were "bearer bonds" without the owner's name printed upon them, which permitted any possessor to receive either dividends or full face value. To short-circuit Tumblety's suit, Boardman & Boardman hired detectives Charles Frost and Charles Chambers to dig up dirt on him. The dossier they compiled persuaded him to drop the matter.

William Burr provided this account of George Lyons' suit against Tumblety.

The son brought a suit against the doctor for atrocious assault, and the evidence collected was of the most disgusting sort. ... I had seen (Tumblety) before that time hovering about the old post office building, where there were many clerks. He had a seeming mania for the company of young men ... I had a big batch of letters sent by him to Lyons, and they were the most confusing farrago of nonsense. Here is one written from the West. He never failed to warn his correspondents against lewd women, and in doing it used the most shocking language.[21]

Opening arguments for the "atrocious assault" case, Lyons vs. Sumblety (sic), took place on July 24, 1880. But this action ultimately collapsed for lack of corroborating evidence.

George Lyons soon began to self-destruct. He worked for a while as a singer in Kerrigan's Star and Garter Bar on Sixth St., long disreputable as an underworld hangout. In the summer of 1881 he ran afoul the law by committing break-ins with two accomplices, perhaps House of Refuge classmates. The New York Sun related what occurred under the heading "Said to be a Son of Ned and Sophie Lyons."

> Several unoccupied houses in the Ninth Ward have been robbed in the past three months by boys who entered them by way of coal chutes. On Monday night Detectives Flanagan and Dilks caught Charles Keutz, Thomas Morris, and George Lyons in the act of robbing a house at 118 West Twelfth St. They learned ... that the same boys had stolen silverware and clothing from 144 West Twelfth St. and 162 West Thirteenth St. At Jefferson Market yesterday, the young prisoners were remanded. Detective Dilks says that George Lyons is the son of Sophie Lyons the shoplifter and confidence woman, and Ned Lyons, the burglar who on the night of July 30 was shot while committing a burglary in South Windham, Connecticut ...[22]

On September 19, 1881, in New York City's Court of General Sessions, George Lyons pled guilty to attempted burglary. Judge Smyth sentenced him to Elmira Reformatory. George did not help himself by audibly muttering that he'd rather go to adult prison, or be hung, than waste any more time in "juvey."

On September 22nd, George entered Elmira Reformatory. At that time Sophie was otherwise occupied. She traveled to Cleveland to pick pockets with long-time accomplice John Larney during assassinated President James Garfield's crowd-lined funeral procession.

George Lyons' file at Elmira described him as uneducated, dishonest, "bright, but thoroughly criminal"[23] and corrupted by a bad upbringing. Capricious superintendent Zebulon Reed Brockway (1827–1920) ran that facility with an iron fist. Though he implemented progressive measures such as work release, parole, vocational training, Christian morals instruction, and military drills, Brockway also firmly believed in corporal punishment. He never spared the rod with recalcitrant inmates.

George declared that Brockway and a guard had once severely beaten him, then assigned him to the reformatory's dangerous foundry, where he was forced "to carry a sixty pound ladle full of molten iron, but was unable to do so without slopping it on his feet and burning them."[24] To punish him for unsatisfactory work performance, Brockway then slammed George in solitary confinement, where he was "shackled to the wall, … fed only bread and … water …,"[25] and left to urinate and defecate in a bucket. George portrayed Brockway as a Jekyll-Hyde figure to an agent of the New York State Assembly. "One minute he would laugh at you, (the next) he'd kill you—very treacherous."[26]

The New York State Board of Charities' 1893 investigation concurred with George's negative assessment of Brockway. According to its report:

> The charges and allegations against General Superintendent
> Z. R. Brockway of cruel, brutal, excessive, degrading, and
> unusual punishment of … inmates are proven and most amply
> sustained by the evidence, and … he is guilty of the same.[27]

Despite the Board's condemnation, Brockway retained his supervisory position until retiring seven years later. He went on to become mayor of Elmira, New York in 1905.

Sophie had other problems besides George in 1882. She was in and out of jail, and had stopped paying St. Mary's Academy for her daughters' tuitions. The nuns in charge soon transferred Florence and Lottie to London, Ontario's Catholic orphanage. When Sophie traveled up to see them, she found out that merchant John Doyle and his wife Mary Catherine had adopted seven year old Lottie. Although Doyle fought Sophie's attempts to reclaim the girl, she eventually succeeded in kidnapping her daughter and fleeing back to Detroit. Because kids got on her nerves, she wasted little time before shipping Lottie off to another boarding school.

Fourteen year old Florence remained at the Sisters of St. Joseph's orphanage in London, Ontario.

On another trip to Canada, Sophie visited Victor at Assumption boarding school. She discovered that he'd been maltreated by the headmaster who learned of her criminal record, and denounced Victor as "a good-for-nothing brat among honest children."[28] According to the account in her book Crime Does Not Pay, she gave the "professor" a tongue-lashing, and accused him of patronizing brothels in Detroit. Whether that's fact or fiction, Sophie did withdraw Victor from the school and brought him home.

Being short of funds, Sophie soon left Detroit to pull off some heists. She left Victor in the custody of a barber named Wilson who owed her money. This double-crosser tried to turn the boy against her by taking him down to the central police station and pointing out Sophie's mug shot. Traumatized Victor soon wound up in the Ladies Christian Union's Home for the Friendless.

Enter Theresa Lewis
During one of her terms in jail Sophie met Theresa White Lewis, a young widow who'd volunteered to read bible passages to prisoners. Theresa came

from a good Detroit family. Her father, Dr. John C. White, had conducted a thriving medical practice, which enabled his wife and five children to live in style.

Theresa wed George W. Lewis in Louisville, Kentucky on November 8, 1866. The circumstances of this marriage suggest it was an elopement. Shortly thereafter the couple moved to St. Lawrence, New York, where George set up shop as a wholesale liquor merchant. After his premature death in 1873 at age 34, Theresa inherited their savings, house, and its contents, but those assets were not sufficient to support her indefinitely. Four years later she returned to Detroit, where we find her living at 117 St. Antoine St., then 220 Lafayette Avenue (1879). By 1881 she resided with sister Isabelle and her husband Thomas G. Kearney at 164 24th St., two blocks from Sophie's home. Brother-in-law Tom did not get along with Theresa and ordered her to move out before September 1st of that year. (In court Kearney testified that he'd insisted that she leave his residence "at least fifty times."[29]) Theresa walked two blocks over to Sophie's house at 51 23rd St. in late August and asked to lease one of her apartments. Remembering Mrs. Lewis as a religious counselor at Detroit House of Corrections, Sophie rented out the front unit of her own duplex to her.

That decision proved to be a regrettable blunder. Though puritanically upright, Theresa was also a busybody. She noticed the coarse characters who came calling at the house, and sensed that Sophie continued to engage in shady undertakings.

The mailman delivered suspicious packages. Most of those parcels were addressed to Sophie's housekeeper Sarah Drew. Theresa took the liberty of opening one box and found three gold watches in it. On September 20th she brought them to Police Superintendent Andrew Rogers, and offered to collect more evidence against Sophie if Rogers would agree to pay her as an undercover agent. Anxious to shut down Mrs. Lyons' theft ring, Rogers ill-advisedly consented to this plan.

Police investigated and discovered that the watches intercepted by Theresa Lewis had been stolen at the Washnetaw County Fair in Ann Arbor. Their rightful owners were Mrs. Harriet Cornwell, Mrs. James Sheldon, and Ms. Fannie Zack. Detroit's Assistant District Attorney James Caplis arraigned Sophie for larceny.

After discovering that Theresa had been spying on her, Sophie literally kicked her out of the house. A few days later she pounded on the Kearneys' front door and insisted upon checking Theresa's trunk for missing items. Either Thomas or Isabelle Kearney let her in. Sophie produced "missing" pieces of jewelry (which she likely brought with her,) claimed that Theresa had filched them, and reported her to police. (A subsequent court hearing exonerated Mrs. Lewis.)

On the morning of February 6, 1882, Sophie and Theresa Lewis ran into one another at Michigan Central Railroad Depot on Woodward St. Both were on their way to Ann Arbor for the opening of Sophie's trial. The Detroit Free Press recounted what happened next.

> Mrs. Lyons approached (Theresa) and claimed that a pair of gloves which she had on her hands were stolen from her ... Mrs. Lewis denied the allegations and an excited war of words ensued which culminated with face scratching and hair pulling, each being determined that the other should get the worst of it. The night watchman at the depot interfered and separated the women ...[30]

The jury returned a guilty verdict in Sophie's March 1882 trial. Judge Joslin sentenced her to five years in prison, with one month credit given for time served. On April 11, 1882, while imprisoned, she was charged for stealing another four watches during President Garfield's funeral in late September 1881.

Sophie remained caged in Detroit House of Corrections for seven months while attorney Colonel John Atkinson appealed to Michigan Supreme Court on her behalf. The court overturned her conviction. However, a second trial in February 1883 resulted in another guilty verdict—also reversed by Michigan Supreme Court. The jury at her third trial in March 1884 found her not guilty.

Theresa Lewis's cantankerous behavior on the witness stand contributed to that unexpected outcome. Although members of Lewis's church had attested to her good character, others perceived her as a snooping troublemaker. Detroit policeman Jesse Williams judged Theresa's reputation mixed—good in some circles, bad in others. Patrolman Manning testified that he wouldn't believe Mrs. Lewis if she had a personal interest in any particular matter. Theresa's unauthorized seizure of Sophie's mail did not sit well with some jurors, nor did her refusal to surrender the thick notebook she kept which recorded detailed information about other people's business. While being cross-examined by Sophie's lawyer, Colonel John Atkinson, Theresa accused him of malfeasance. She claimed to have overheard Atkinson in an Ann Arbor hotel lobby telling colleagues that he'd secured his fee from Sophie with liens on two of her properties, along with some "hot" watches. Atkinson denied those allegations. At the direction of Judge Joslin he issued a signed affidavit refuting her accusations, which was read at the next court session.

In contrast to self-righteous Theresa, Sophie provided a bit of humor, testifying that,

All the property identified (as stolen) is (mine). The opera
glass ... I bought ten years ago. I lost (a) ... watch ... While
Mrs. Lewis was at my house I told her of (its disappearance),
but did not accuse her, as she was always praying. (Laughter)
She prayed every night, and ... persuaded me to do so ... I did
not see Mrs. Lewis take a thing. (But) I found my fur coat in
(her) sister's house. It was in a trunk.[31]

Theresa Lewis deemed herself a civic-minded whistle-blower. Sophie
viewed her not only as a snitch, the criminal fraternity's lowest caste of
humanity, but a hypocritical ingrate, whom she'd tried to help. In addition
to nearly ruining her, Mrs. Lewis caused collateral damage to Sophie's
friends Bob McKinney, "Big Ed" Rice, and Emmanuel "Minnie" Marx,
all of whom did time because Theresa ratted on them. Even Police Chief
Andrew Rogers suffered from his association with her. Mayor William
G. Thompson fired Rogers for putting Mrs. Lewis on the city payroll as a
"detective" (but later rehired him).

Embittered crime-stopper Theresa Lewis died of cancer in St. Mary's
hospital at the age of 44 on May 11, 1886. She claimed that Sophie Lyons'
assault in February, 1882 had energized the dormant malignancy in her
body to an aggressively lethal condition. Though Theresa's contempt for
privacy and First Amendment rights overstepped the bounds of legal pro-
priety, her recovery of stolen watches proved Sophie's involvement in the
Ann Arbor fair thefts beyond doubt.

George Lyons' Fate

Busy Sophie Lyons paid only one visit to son George at Elmira Reformatory.
He irately demanded she get him out of there. When Sophie attempted
to explain she didn't have the power do that, he yelled: "God pity me if I
ever see you alive again!"[32] Nineteen year old George, stuck in his own hell,

simply hadn't matured enough to comprehend the hardships his mother faced.

His wish for the company of hardened criminals came true on December 19, 1885 when New York's Department of Corrections transferred him to Auburn State Prison. Unfortunately, George died there of typhoid fever on February 2, 1886, seven months short of his September release date. He was buried four days later at St. Joseph's Cemetery in Fleming, New York.

In an interview with the New York World ten years later, Sophie declared:

> Only one son came to grief. He was arrested because ... of a college row—never mind when or where—and he died in prison. Even when he was a convict I did not desert him. ... I gave him a decent burial and alone followed him to the grave.[33]

As we know, George did not go to prison because of a "college row." At the time of his death, Ned Lyons had landed back in jail, and Sophie incurred substantial legal fees as a result of three successive trials. Ned's old friend "Big Jim" Brady, then incarcerated at Auburn, had befriended young George. He paid for his final expenses, not Sophie.

Endnotes

1 New York World, November 19, 1888.

2 Sophie Lyons, Why Crime Does Not Pay, The Star Co., J. S. Ogilvie Publishing Co. New York, NY, 1913, pp. 16-17.

3 Shayne Davidsuon, Queen of the Burglars: The Scandalous Life of Sophie Lyons, Exposit Books, Jefferson, North Carolina, 2020, p. 125.

4 Ibid.

5 Ibid., p. 140, op. cit. Detroit Free Press, August 16, 1908.

6 The 1880 U. S. census lists Sophie's family in Detroit as "George English," 45 years old, "money broker," 51 23rd St., Detroit, Michigan, Sophia, 29, keeping house, George 14, Florence 11, Victoria (sic) 6, Lottie 5, Mable 4. "George English" was one of Ned Lyons' aliases. He sired George, Florence, Eugenia, and possibly Victor. (However, Victor's death certificate stated that his father was Edward Mason, which might refer to New York criminal Edward Ryan, aka Edward "Tammany" Mason.) There has been speculation that the biological father of Lottie was burglar "Dutch Fred" Bennett. Some suspected Hamilton Brock of being Mable's progenitor. Jealous hubby Ned evidently thought so since he precipitated a shoot-out with Ham at Kerrigan's bar on October 24, 1880. Lyons got the worst of it, receiving bullet wounds through his mouth and pectoral, while Brock emerged unscathed. Jim Brady fathered Madeline (who was baptized "Sophia," but always went by the name "Madeline").

7 Thomas F. Byrnes, Professional Criminals of America, Cassell & Co., New York, NY, 1886, p. 204.

8 Ibid., p. 206.

9 Ibid., p. 205.

10 New York Times, February 1, 1880.

11 New York Sun, February 1, 1880.

12 Ibid.

13 Ibid.

14 New York Times, February 1, 1880.

15 Ibid.

16 Ibid.

17 New York Herald, February 2, 1880.

18 Rochester Democrat & Republican, December 3, 1888. William Burr had an office at 320 Broadway; Charles A. Dunham's office was located on the

same block at 335 Broadway. Both of those places were within a block of Tumblety's 1860-1861 quarters at 400 Broadway.

19 Estate of Francis Tumblety Probate Proceedings, statement of Robert H. Simpson, Esq.

20 Rochester Democrat & Republican, December 3, 1888.

21 Ibid.

22 New York Sun, August 31, 1887.

23 Davidson, p. 90, op. cit. Elmira Reformatory Biographical Registers and Receiving Blotters.

24 Ibid., p. 91, op. cit. Documents of the Assembly of New York, 10th Session, 1882, p. 143.

25 Ibid.

26 Ibid.

27 Alexander Pisciotta, Benevolent Repression: Social Control & the American Reformatory Prison Movement, New York University Press, New York, 1994, p. 33, op. cit. Albany State Archives, "Report & Proceedings of the State Board of Charities Relative to the Management of the State Reformatory at Elmira," March 14, 1894 release date.

28 Lyons, p. 24.

29 Detroit Free Press, December 3, 1881.

30 Ibid., February 7, 1882.

31 Ibid., December 3, 1881.

32 Davidson, p. 91, op. cit. Elmira Reformatory Biographical Registers and Receiving Blotters.

33 New York World, June 28, 1896.

CHAPTER 4:

Wayward Attempts to Get Back on Track

During the Lyons trial Tumblety lived under an assumed name at Edward and Mary McNamara's boardinghouse, 77 E. Tenth St. in Manhattan. The 1880 U. S. census listed fifty year old Francis as "James Dombletree," 45, medical doctor, boarder, unmarried, born in Ireland.

Adverse publicity emanating from that scandal further harmed Tumblety's less-than-sterling reputation. According to a New York World article, bartenders and patrons at one of his favorite watering holes, McKenna's Saloon on Fourth Ave. now "spoke of him with loathing and contempt."[1] The 5th Ave. Hotel's detective, James Pryor, ejected Tumblety from the hotel's bar because "the gentlemen (there) did not care to have him near them."[2]

Despite the reputational damage caused by the Lyons' lawsuit, Francis seemed to ramp up his sexual activity. During the fall of 1880 he traveled to Toronto. On the night of October 14th police arrested him on The Esplanade by Lake Ontario for assaulting an adolescent male.

In late February 1881 Tumblety cruised by steamboat to New Orleans for Mardi Gras. He so loved that pagan-Christian festival and the city's anything-goes atmosphere that this pilgrimage would become a ritual for the next twenty years. He would either stay at the four-star St. Charles Hotel, or upscale bed and breakfasts in the French Quarter. That year he boarded in a private townhouse. His landlady witnessed several young males entering his room, some remaining overnight. Neighbors noticed his night-stalker habits, misogyny, and homoerotic proclivities.

> The doctor was known in New Orleans as a pronounced woman hater, (yet) was often seen in the street in the company of ... boys, of whom he was very fond.[3]

While in New Orleans Tumblety met 18 year old telegraph opera-tor Richard S. Norris, and became infatuated with him. After the holiday Francis offered to take Richard on a vacation to Mexico, which he declined. But they would meet up for Mardi Gras annually over the next two decades. (Norris subsequently worked for the New Orleans Police Department as a fingerprint analyst. He married Mary Gitz in 1894, and fathered a son by her.)

On March 22, 1881, custom house employee Henry Govan noticed that his wallet was missing shortly after drinking in a bar with Tumblety. Instead of calling the police, Govan hired private detective Dominick C. O'Malley to handle the case. O'Malley located and arrested Tumblety, then dragged him to the nearest police station, where he was searched, ques-tioned, and released. At the hearing on March 30th Judge Mittenberger heard testimony from Tumblety, Govan, and O'Malley. Sensing the shake-down of a gay tourist, Mittenberger declared Tumblety's arrest unjustified and dismissed charges against him.

Shortly after that ordeal Francis caught a riverboat up the Mississippi to St. Louis, where police wrote him up for impersonating an army doctor. Sometime in July 1882 he returned to New York City, met 17 year old barber Martin H. McGarry, and offered him a secretarial job. McGarry accepted. Posing as the independently wealthy son of an Irish land-owner, and retired Union Army surgeon, Tumblety brought McGarry to

Philadelphia, Saratoga Springs, New Haven, Connecticut, Niagara Falls, Ireland, and England. They stayed together four years, and separated on good terms. With the money he saved during his tenure with Tumblety, McGarry bought an alarm bell, buzzer, and speaking tube business—Caffrey & McGarry, 274 E. Broadway.

Francis and another party filed a lawsuit in London—Tumblety-Smiles vs. Hart—which Lord Justice Bowen decided without jury on July 17, 1886. This action apparently resolved difficulties fugitive-from-justice Tumblety had encountered in trying to sell real estate he owned in Canada.

Business correspondence placed him in Washington, D. C. during May 1887. On June 5th of that year he introduced himself to African-American icon Frederick Douglass on a Liverpool street. Douglass wrote to his friend Amy Kirby Post that he could hardly get a word in edgewise, because Francis never shut up.

Sometime after returning to New York City in October 1887, Tumblety went back Washington. There he allegedly commenced an affair with 28 year old Isaac Edwin Golladay, the nephew of two southern congressmen.

A friend of Golladay wrote this anonymous letter to The Washington Evening Star in November, 1888.

My attention was directed to an article in your paper yesterday regarding the arrest of Dr. Tumblety in London on suspicion of being connected to the Whitechapel murders. The notice revived sad memories of the mysterious disappearance of young Isaac Golliday (sic), whom I had known from childhood ... He often spoke of Dr. Tumblety, and someone told me his father, Frederick Golliday, had tried to break up the friendship between his son and Dr. Tumblety ... If I have been correctly informed, Isaac Golliday left his father's boarding house after dark and was never seen or heard of since. The last conversation I had with his father he had no clue as to his whereabouts. As Dr. Tumblety was not seen in Washington after Isaac's disappearance from home, it was hoped by his friends he had gone to Europe with the doctor and might possibly return ...[4]

Because of Tumblety's voyage to England, Washington police never questioned him about Golladay's mysterious disappearance. Isaac ultimately turned up as a farmer in Lebanon, Tennessee, married to wife Sophia, and living until September 7, 1934.

Francis never formed a long-term relationship with another "confidential valet," following his break-up with Isaac Gollady. Thereafter, his love life consisted mainly of casual rendezvouses with strangers.

Tumblety's book had gone through several editions between 1871 and 1900, expanding from 96 to 156 pages in the process. It should really be classed as a miscellany rather than autobiography. Although Tumblety's 1866 pamphlet "The Kidnapping of Dr. Tumblety" provided a brief and sanitized account of his early life, the later editions of his autobiography revealed virtually nothing about his lowly origins, parents, siblings, or arrest history. Instead readers find exaggerated accounts of Francis's achievements, travels, and philanthropic endeavors, along with his medical philosophy, Irish home-rule opinions, and laudatory testimonials from eminent individuals.

Tumblety practiced alternative medicine via herbal remedies. He abjured blood-letting and the use of toxic agents such as mercury and arsenic to treat diseases. Although critics harped on his failings as a healer, he regularly effected cures, and most of his naturopathic medical beliefs seem sensible. Francis advocated the "salutary evacuation of morbific mat-ter,"[5] and therefore prescribed laxatives such as Dr. Tumblety's Vegetable Compound to "assist nature in removing obstruction(s) ..."[6] Indigestion and constipation caused food to rot in the stomach, thus engendering maladies ranging from the common cold to cancer. Tumblety's hypothesis loosely corresponds with that of contemporary medical pundits who have linked multitudinous ailments to a "leaky gut." Francis thought toxemia from dyspepsia and irregularity could lead to terminal cancer, heart dis-ease, hypertension, and diabetes, as well as psychological disorders such as irritability, melancholia, nervousness, and misanthropy.

Besides stressing the importance of purging one's body of impurities, Tumblety preached the benefits of exercise and necessity of avoiding over-work. He recommended bicycling to counteract "torpid liver."

> The act of pedaling the cycle instantly quickens circulation in
> the feet and legs, and in ... a quarter ... hour sends a torrent of
> blood through the veins of the legs and pelvis into the portal
> vein, which spreads itself out of the liver from the lower side.
> In other words, the effect of cycling upon the liver is the same
> as that of flooding a still and stagnant lake with innumerable
> mountain streams after a heavy rainfall ...[7]

Tumblety compared the processes of digestion and assimilation to alchemy. The usable essence of food—or "chyle"—miraculously regener-ated the human organism by producing new cells.

> Natural alchemy separates the useful elements from food
> (entering) the stomach, transforms it into chyle, and blood
> into muscles, bones, (etc.) and rejects that which is useless.[8]

Tumblety wrote:

Our bodies are always undergoing change, (ceaselessly) wearing and wasting away, and constantly supplied and repaired by food, drink, and air ... By this gradual change of particles it is estimated that the soft parts of our bodies become entirely changed in the space of one year and our bones in seven years.[9]

However, the human body gradually loses this magical ability to rejuvenate itself. Francis wrote: "To grow old itself is a disease."[10] Aging stems from the deterioration of one's regenerative powers.

To illustrate the dangers of being a sedentary workaholic, Francis penned a subchapter entitled "Great Men Who Died of Overwork." I will quote two of his anecdotes about high-achievers who died prematurely from "underworking the muscles and overworking the brain."[11]

When Hon. Daniel Manning (1831-1887) came to Washington from Albany his eye was bright, his step steady. His massive frame worked like that of a skilled athlete. ... When he took hold of the Treasury Department (for President Grover Cleveland), he threw his whole soul into it. He dropped his exercise to devote more time to it, and studied on night and day until the demon of overwork grabbed him, and he fell down in his office (from) an apoplectic fit.[12]

Noted Ohio statesman Tom Corwin's death occurred at a reception in Washington. Corwin (1794-1865) had just returned from his mission in Mexico and was chatting with a crowd of men ... He was the life of the assemblage. When a friend came over and shook his hand, Corwin quipped: 'You are more bald than when I last saw you, but then Caesar was bald.' 'Yes,' replied the man, 'but Caesar had fits.' At this remark Corwin became serious and said: 'Twenty years ago I saw a man fall unconscious from a paralytic stroke. He was in the midst of excited discourse, and was carried out of the hall by his friends insensible. The first act of consciousness he showed ... was to utter the words you just said, 'Caesar had fits.' A few minutes later (Corwin) was in the refreshment room, surrounded by a crowd, when his voice suddenly sunk to a whisper, and he reached forth his hands, asking for air ... A few moments later he was dead.[13]

In his "Philosophy of Life" essay Tumblety discussed psychosomatic illness. He firmly believed that pessimistic thinking undermined health. To provide an example, he described an experiment conducted by unethical Russian scientists on four men condemned to death.

Two of them were placed in beds where other persons had died of cholera, without knowing the fact, but no effect was produced upon them. The other men were placed in clean beds, but were told that others had died in those beds of cholera, and that this was the means by which they were to be executed. The effect on their imaginations was so great that in a few hours, they both died.[14]

On the other hand, a positive attitude promoted physical wellbeing. Tumblety knew of the placebo effect sixty years before Harvard researcher Dr. Henry K. Beecher popularized it. In the 1893 edition of his autobiography Francis touted the benefits of "posi-tude":

Many ... find the 'balm of all their woes' in cod liver oil or some other popular nostrum. With such it makes little difference what is administered, provided it is harmless to the system ... It's well known that a patient is much more likely to receive benefit from the medicine he takes if he has confidence in its virtue, (and) believes it will cure him.[15]

As early as the 1870's Tumblety railed against air and water pollution. He deplored the proliferation of factory smoke in the atmosphere and discharge of toxic chemicals into bodies of water. Francis disapproved of lax zoning practices which permitted sewage plants and garbage dumps to be situated near residential areas. He recommended more parks in urban areas since trees counterbalanced mammalian pollution by absorbing carbon dioxide and exhaling oxygen. He contended that zoos, "with their "foul odors,"[16] defeated the beneficial effects of parks.

Tumblety drank beer and wine, but generally avoided distilled spirits. Valet Martin McGarry remembered him sometimes having a pint of ale with breakfast. When hypochondriac Hall Caine thought he'd contracted some dreadful disease in 1875, Francis gave him packets of pills and advised him to wash them down with three or four glasses of stout. Tumblety was known to buy champagne and other wines by the case. Nevertheless, he adamantly opposed the production of bootleg liquors and adulterated foods. Convinced that alcoholism accelerated aging, he wrote: "Drunkards don't live out half their days."[17] The abuses of unprincipled distillers made some booze lethal. While living in New York City he paid a laboratory to ascertain the ingredients of several brands of liquor, then published the alarming test results.

In the sample of 'pure Holland gin' we found neutral spirits, rotten corn, juniper berries, turpentine, vitriol. We dropped the white of an egg and an oyster ... into this compound and saw them shrivel into hard stringy masses ..." In 'fine old handmade Kentucky whiskey' we found neutral spirits, glycerine, sulfate of zinc, chromic acid, creosote, unslacked lime, and fusel oil. ... In port wine we found neutral acid, glycerine, licorice, zinc, mercury, antimony, salts of tartar, ether, muriatic acid, and alum.[18]

Cheers!

In spite of such advanced views, Tumblety still clung to the ancient Greeks' sanguine-choleric-melancholy-phlegmatic theory of temperaments, and physiognomy, the pseudo-science which equated facial features with personality traits.

Coarseness, cruelty, vanity, and shallowness betray themselves, while kindness, culture, and refinement of the spiritual life will transform the most ordinary (face).[19]

Perhaps because adversaries labelled him a crank, Tumblety strained to put a positive spin on that pejorative term. To him it meant an independent non-conformist with original ideas, who repudiated the platitudes of conventional society. He posited the untenable thesis that,

Cranks are instrumental in the onward movement of the world. Julius Caesar, Napoleon, George Washington, Carlyle, Lincoln, and Bismarck were all cranks ... He who has the individuality, the force of character to think for himself, and sufficient manly independence to care not for public opinion ... generally enjoys good health.[20]

Dictionaries define "crank" as a crackpot who stubbornly adheres to odd or discredited notions. Such individuals often disrespect legal precedent and Judeo-Christian values. Most of us agree that Maximilian Robespierre, Vladimir Illych Lenin, and Adolf Hitler were cranks, but not Washington, Carlyle, or Lincoln.

Francis Tumblety possessed the "Gift of Blarney." Because of his natural eloquence, members of Montreal's Irish community tapped him to run against Thomas D'Arcy McGee for a parliament seat in December, 1857. Though he declined that honor, Tumblety remained something of a fixture on the Irish banquet circuit. At the end of his autobiography Francis published excerpts from a speech he delivered in Boston circa 1868.

> To (English) penal laws (against Ireland) America owes one-third of her population. The same (Irish) race ... furnished Washington with one-half of his army... Lord Mountjoy in the House of Commons told the ministry: 'You have lost America through the Irish.' Washington himself, when he became a member of The Friendly Sons of St. Patrick publicly acknowledged ... indebtedness to Ireland.[21]

When ticking off Irish heroes of the Revolutionary War such as General John Sullivan, "Mad Anthony" Wayne, and General John Stark, Tumblety mentioned naval commander John Barry.

> Commodore Barry, the Wexford boy, Father of the American Navy," who on encountering an English fleet was asked by a surly captain, 'What ship is that?' and replied, 'The U. S. ship Alliance, Saucy Jack Barry, half Irishman. Who the hell are you?' He then and there attacked the British fleet, destroyed two of their ships and put the rest to flight.[22]

Tumblety packed his book with plugs from famous men, grateful patients, businesses he patronized, and upstanding people who just happened to like his better self.

According to Francis, President Abraham Lincoln wrote a letter of introduction on his behalf addressed to British Foreign Secretary Lord John Russell.

> Dear Sir—The bearer of this, Francis Tumblety M.D., an esteemed friend of mine, is about to visit London for the first time, and will consequently be a stranger to your metropolis. Any attention which you may extend to him will be greatly appreciated by Your friend and humble servant, A. Lincoln.[23]

Tumblety claimed to have met Lincoln. Although that seems unlikely, a more plausible story has it that he crossed paths with Mary Todd Lincoln and her son Robert at a Long Branch, New Jersey resort in August 1861, and treated Robert for a sprained ankle.

Upon receiving a copy of Tumblety's book about his 1865 arrest in St. Louis, General Robert E. Lee wrote:

> My Dear Sir—I have received this morning the pamphlet giving some passages of your life, with your letter of the 18th instant. The former I will take the earliest opportunity to read, and for the latter, please accept my thanks. Very respectfully, your obedient servant, R. E. Lee.[24]

General William Tecumseh Sherman also acknowledged receipt of The Kidnapping of Dr. Tumblety.

Dear Sir—Yours of July 9th was duly received, and while I regret the indignity and suffering to which you were subjected, I am sorry that it is entirely out of my province to aid you in obtaining the satisfaction which such a case undoubtedly merits. With great respect, etc. W.T. Sherman, Lieutenant-General.[25]

On September 18, 1872, former Emperor Louis Napoleon III allegedly wrote Francis from Cowles on The Island of Wight: "I was much touched, sir, by the amiable letter that you addressed to me and by the sentiments you have offered … in my misfortune. I wish, therefore, today, to thank you for the sympathy you have shown me, and to assure you of my distinguished sentiments. Napoleon."[26]

Tumblety also published endorsements from newspaper editor Horace Greeley, poet Henry Wadsworth Longfellow, and "Autocrat of the Breakfast Table" Dr. Oliver Wendell Holmes. Longfellow's thank-you note, dated July 12, 1887, stated:

My Worthy Friend: I have received your letter containing the memento you received from the hands of England's poet laureate Baron Tennyson for which I am extremely thankful. The memento is an original verse from the great Englishman, and the subject is gratitude. One of the first lessons taught me is that gratitude is one of man's noblest attributes. I believe this to be true, and have never forgotten it. Hence, accept my thanks both for the (poem) in Tennyson's handwriting and for your thoughtful kindness. Sincerely yours, Henry W. Longfellow.[27]

As Tumblety chronicler Timothy Riordan pointed out, Longfellow died on March 24, 1882, and Alfred Lord Tennyson was not made a Baron by Queen Victoria until 1883. This makes us wonder about the authenticity of letters Tumblety produced from Lincoln, Napoleon III, Benjamin Disraeli, Charles Dickens, etc.

Multiple plagiarisms have been identified in Tumblety's book. Timothy Riordan credibly asserted that some parts of the travelogues were copied from long lost 19th Century tour guides. Michael Hawley recognized unattributed passages from the writings of Thomas Jefferson, herbalist Samuel Thomson, and Thomson's disciple A. R. Porter.

Among the businesses which endorsed Tumblety were: Williams & Guinon (ship owners), Hudnut's Pharmacy, banker Henry Clews, H. Alberst (boot and shoe merchant), and the two bathhouses he frequented: Dr. C. T. Ryan's Lafayette Baths and Dr. E. P Miller's Sanitarium. He also garnered testimonials from Congressman John J. O'Neill, lawyer Daniel J. Rooney, Esq., and Grand Central Hotel Manager W. H. Guernsey. Some of these letters have the perfunctory ring of thanking a customer for his patronage.

Personal friends who vouched for Tumblety included Brooklyn landlord Elisha Hanshew, Father A. Hoecken of Xavier College in Cincinnati, Methodist minister Rev. W. H. De Puy, whom he met on a transatlantic voyage, sculptor Wilson MacDonald, and satisfied patient John A. Best of Washington, PA. Elisha Hanshew declared: "This is to certify that I have known Dr. Tumblety for twenty-four years. I knew him only as a gentleman, honorable and upright."[28] On January 2, 1883, Reverend De Puy wrote:

I well remember the incident connected with our first acquaintance on board the (ship) City of Rome ... to the Old World ... (It) soon ripened into a sincere friendship which has continued until the present time. I need not add that during your stay in this city I shall be glad to have you call at my office as often as may suit your convenience. I remain, my dear sir, very truly yours, Rev. W. H. De Puy, D.D., LL.D.[29]

Tumblety's opponents tended to ignore his charitable streak. In Buffalo, Toronto, New York City, and elsewhere people remembered him throwing coins to street urchins. On February 22, 1859, he donated twenty barrels of flour to the poor in Buffalo. Over the years Francis contributed significant sums to Catholic hospitals and religious orders. But those benevolent acts were not enough to clear his name.

Endnotes

1 New York World, November 17, 1888.

2 Pittsburgh Daily Chronicle & Telegraph, November 27, 1888.

3 St. Louis Post Dispatch, June 28, 1903.

4 Washington Evening Star, November 21, 1888.

5 Francis Tumblety M.D., A Sketch of the Life of Dr. Francis Tumblety, Presenting an Outline of his Wonderful Career as Physician, Brooklyn, New York, 1893, p. 7. (Like the 1889 edition, this one was self-published. Tumblety paid The Brooklyn Eagle newspaper's print shop to do the typesetting and printing.)

6 Ibid., p. 10.

7 Ibid. p. 144.

8 Ibid., p. 233.

9 Ibid., pp. 125 – 126.

10 Ibid., p. 131.

11 Ibid., 130.

12 Ibid., p. 133.

13 Ibid., p. 136.

14 Ibid., p. 123.

15 Ibid., p. 124.

16 Ibid., p. 89.

17 Ibid., p. 87.

18 Ibid., p. 142.

19 Ibid., p. 141.

20 Ibid., p. 146.

21 Ibid., pp. 151-154.

22 Ibid., p. 153.

23 Ibid. p. 21 letter of recommendation from Abraham Lincoln dated April 13, 1863.

24 Ibid. p. 22, letter from Robert E. Lee to Francis Tumblety dated May 24, 1869.

25 Ibid., p. 22, letter from Lt. Gen. William E. Sherman to Francis Tumblety dated July 20, 1868.

26 Ibid., 44, letter from former Emperor Napoleon III to Francis Tumblety dated September 18, 1872.

27 Ibid., p. 109, alleged letter from Henry Wadsworth Longfellow, dated July 12, 1887. (Tumblety biographer Timothy Riordan pointed out the fact that Longfellow died five years earlier on March 24, 1882.)

28 Ibid., p. 95, undated testimonial letter from Tumblety's landlord Elisha Hanshew, 567 Quincy St., Brooklyn, NY.

29 Ibid., January 2, 1883 letter from Rev. W. H. De Puy to Francis Tumblety.

CHAPTER 5

Tumblety's Ill-Fated English Sojourn

Tumblety sailed to England in May 1888. After renting a room in West London, he actively sought the company of gay and bisexual young men. London Metropolitan Police charged him for four separate acts of "gross indecency" committed on July 27th, August 31st, October 8th, and November 2nd. They identified his sex partners as Albert Fisher (July 27th), John Doughty, Arthur Brice, and James Crowley. Those encounters were most likely consensual for pay. At that time the meaning of "gross indecency" between two males in England was heavy petting, even to the point of mutual ejaculation, without committing sodomy. (Penalties for sodomy were more severe.)

Tumblety's bedmates were all twenty-something working class males who made side money as rent boys. Various censuses listed their occupations as laborer (Fisher and Doughty), general service (i.e., servant, Brice), and "harbor" (i.e., stevedore, Crowley.) In later years there were several poor-law workhouse admissions for three of those men (Arthur Brice excepted.)

Police detained Tumblety for questioning about the Whitechapel murders on October 1st and released him two days later. Coppers turned Tumblety's London apartment upside down, but did not discover bloody clothing, knives, or any other evidence. What they did find were salacious letters exchanged between him and his male sex partners.. According to The London Post,

> Dr. Tumblety was afterwards taken into custody on another
> charge, arising out of certain correspondence with young

men found in his possession, and ... committed for trial at the Old Bailey."[1]

On the evening of November 7, 1888 London Metropolitan Police detectives arrested Tumblety for sexual offenses. After interrogation, they hauled him before police magistrate James L. Hannay, who remanded him to Holloway Prison. According to Marlboro Street Police Court records, Tumblety was not bailed out until November 14th. On that date Judge Hannay scheduled a Central Criminal Court hearing for November 16th, and set bail at 300 pounds (the equivalent of $33,000. dollars today). Tumblety paid his bond on the 14th and was released. Although that sum was high for an indecency offense, Hannay would have held Francis without bail if he thought him guilty of the Whitechapel murders.) Note that Tumblety's incarceration between November 7th and the 14th made it impossible for him to have murdered Mary Jane Kelly on November 9th.)

Through its English sources, The Cincinnati Enquirer learned that London police were more interested in one of Tumblety's associates.

> From information which leaked out yesterday around police headquarters, the inquiries here are not so much in reference to Tumblety himself as to a companion who attracted almost as much attention as the doctor, both on account of the oddity of his character and the shadow-like persistence with which he followed his employer.[2]

One of the individuals to whom Tumblety wrote off-color notes might have been the medical school intern, allegedly born and raised in Philadelphia, who also collected uterus specimens. Twenty years later newspaper columnist George R. Sims wrote:

(One) theory puts the (crimes) down to a young American medical student who was in London during the whole time of the murders, and ... who made on two occasions an endeavor to obtain a certain internal organ, which for his purposes had to be removed from the almost living body.[3]

The medical student in question might have been influenced by Dr. Charles-Edouard Brown-Sequard, a pioneer endocrinologist who claimed to have revived himself by injecting fresh animal fluids, including one derived from monkey testicles.

The Chicago Tribune picked up the following dispatch from New York World's London correspondent:

An eminent engineer in London suggested to police the theory that the murderer was a medical maniac trying to find the elixir of life and was looking for the essential ingredient in parts taken from murdered bodies.[4]

The Dead End on Batty Street

Some "Ripperologists" have tried to link this mysterious intern to "the Batty Street Lodger." Mrs. Kuers, the German-born wife of a seaman, operated a boardinghouse at 22 Batty St. in London's Whitechapel district. As a sideline, she took in laundry from single men. On September 30th, shortly after Elizabeth Stride and Catherine Eddowes had been brutally murdered, one of her customers dropped off clothing to be washed, which included blood-stained wristbands and shirts. He also left behind a black leather medical bag.

Mrs. Kuers had two long-term male tenants: Joseph, a brewery's horse-drawn wagon driver, and baker Carl Noun, who took long leaves of absence while working in the resort town of Margate between May and October. Mrs. Kuers might have seen nothing wrong with letting out Mr. Noun's quarters to short-term roomers while he was away.

On or about October 1st, while lugging a basket of dirty laundry to her back yard sink, Mrs. Kuers greeted the lady next door, and complained about the bloody shirt and cuffs one of her clients had dumped onto her lap. How on earth would she be able to get them clean again? She immediately regretted opening her mouth, since her neighbor instantly began prattling about that man's possible involvement with the double murder which just occurred around the corner in Mitre Square. She reminded Mrs. Kuers of her civic duty, and urged her to report this evidence to the authorities.

Mrs. Kuers reluctantly contacted Metropolitan Police. Detectives questioned her and took both the bloody clothing and medical bag into custody. The bag contained medical instruments, ticket stubs marked "Liverpool," obscene pictures, and other miscellaneous items. Mrs. Kuers added to the confusion by mentioning in her heavy German accent that the bloodstained articles might have belonged to another laundry customer, the ladies' fashion designer of foreign extraction who worked for a posh West End establishment.

Plainclothes detectives staked out 22 Batty St. and nabbed the medical student on October 6th, when he arrived to pick up his washed clothing. They brought the doctor in for interrogation, and held him in jail. His alibis evidently held up, since he was cleared, and released on October 9th. Perhaps miffed that Mrs. Kuers reported him to the authorities as the Whitechapel serial killer, he never reclaimed his clothing or medical bag.

About this time Mrs. Kuers' long-term tenant Carl Noun returned. She worried he would be displeased by the uproar, and seek other quarters. Mr. Noun might not have been overjoyed that she allowed a suspected murderer to sleep in his bed, but he put it in perspective. From years of experience he knew that Mrs. Kuers was not the kind of person who would knowingly rent out rooms short-term to any maniac with two quid in his pocket.

An article in The London Evening News described Mrs Kuers as a "stout" old woman who spoke "very bad English," and 22 Batty St. as a dilapidated flophouse. Offended that his landlady and abode had been portrayed in such a derogatory manner, Carl Noun rose to Mrs. Kuers' defense by writing a letter of protest to the paper.

Sir,

Referring to your issue #2227, I beg of you to publish a contradictory statement respecting the Whitechapel murder(s). In fact your reporter has been wrongly informed, or else it is his own suggestion. The police are not in the house, nor has the woman had a lodger, who is now missing, but a stranger brought in the shirts, and when he fetched them, he was detained by the police and after inquiries discharged. As regards our (residence), it is not as your report describes it, (but) ... a most respectable house, and in good general condition; although it is certainly not Windsor Castle. There are only two lodgers, one a drayman, name of Joseph, who works for the Norwegian Lager Beer Co., and the other a baker, name of Carl Noun, who has been at work in Margate, and only returned the 6th of this month after the season was over. I trust you will publish these statements ... (Otherwise), it may injure the poor woman in her business.

Respectfully,

Carl Noun[5]

To my knowledge, no one has satisfactorily identified the enigmatic Batty Street "Lodger," much less proven him a body parts dealer or one of Francis Tumblety's lovers. Years later, in 1907, Mrs. Kuers told a newspaper reporters that this same individual then conducted a prosperous medical practice in northwest London.

Tumblety's Ambivalence Toward Surgery

Much has been made of Tumblety's medical background, but his knowledge of anatomy and surgery was limited. Although he posed as a surgeon to Martin McGarry and General McClellan's staff, Francis actually spurned both blood-letting and surgery. In his autobiography he condemned the scalpel as a "source of immense mischief to the human family.[6] Tumblety copied the first stanza of his advertising motto from Samuel Thomson's poem "Lobelia Speaks for Itself," which proclaimed:

> We use such balms as have no strife
> With Nature or the laws of life;
> With blood our hands we never stain,
> Nor poison men to ease their pain.[7]

Even Police Inspector John G. Littlechild admitted that Francis Tumblety was "not a known sadist."[8] Blood and guts made him woozy. He would have delegated the evisceration of women to miscreants with stronger stomachs. Like Edinburgh anatomist Dr. Robert Knox who patronized homicidal grave robbers William Burke and William Hare, Tumblety paid for organ specimens without asking awkward questions about their provenance.

Although detectives judged Tumblety too tall, old, gimpy, and squeamish to be the Ripper, some thought he might be in league with him. Francis sought compounds extracted from female body parts to treat his neuralgia and syphilitic arthritis. Unethical morticians, doctors, "resurrection men," or even murderers might have supplied those "goods".

One theory hypothesized that Tumblety conspired with the Viktor-Frankenstein-like Batty Street Lodger to cut out uteri from fresh female corpses, then blend them with other arcane ingredients into a witches' brew designed to transform him back into a healthy 25 year old.

Michael Hawley observed that the Ripper excised uteri, a kidney, and heart from victims.

> In the same year as the murders (Tumblety) feared his kidney and heart disease might cause him sudden death. His preoccupation with these three organs is clear.[9]

No concoctions which might have been derived from animal or human organs cured Tumblety's rheumatism or the wart-like growths on his face. In the 1893 edition of his autobiography he confessed that there was no such thing as an "elixir of life."

On November 17th The New York World's London correspondent E. Tracy Greaves wrote an article disclosing that U. S. resident Francis "Twomblety" (sic) was suspected by Metropolitan Police of being involved in the Whitechapel murders. (The Boston Globe incorrectly printed Francis's last name as "Kumblety.")

On November 19th, a grand jury decided there was enough evidence to put Francis on trial for gross indecency. If found guilty on all four counts, he would likely have received a sentence of eight years hard labor.

Based on past experience, Tumblety deeply mistrusted the entire criminal justice system, composed of cops, lawyers, judges, and prison guards. He'd not fared well in the Portmore malpractice case of 1859, or when Philadelphia's constabulary expelled him from that city in June 1863, nor the time St. Louis Provost Marshal J. D. Baker arrested him in 1865 on suspicion of being a conspirator in President Lincoln's assassination. Judges and jurors tended to look askance at Tumblety. Besides, he'd been up to no good in London: cavorting with rent boys by night, while spending his daylight hours selling quack remedies, and trying to relieve his venereal disease with extracts from black market body parts.

On November 23, 1888, four days after the grand jury's decision to try him, Tumblety fled to Boulogne, France. He bolted due to the possibility of doing eight years hard labor for "unnatural offences," not because he perpetrated the Ripper murders. Under the alias "Frank Townsend," Tumblety sailed from Le Havre on November 24th aboard the steamer La Bretagne, bound for New York City. That would be his last trans-Atlantic voyage.

On December 2nd New York City plainclothesmen met the La Bretagne as it docked. Detectives Hickey and Crowley surveilled Tumblety as he disembarked from the gangplank with his trunk at 1:30 PM, and kept him under observation. Soon almost everyone in Manhattan knew that he "hid out" in one of his old haunts: Mrs. Mary McNamara's boardinghouse at 77-79 E. Tenth St. Reporters asked Mrs. McNamara, whom they bluntly described as "a fat, good-natured old lady,"[10] if having a boarder accused of the Whitechapel atrocities made her uneasy. She answered: "Dr. Tumblety is a perfect gentleman. He wouldn't hurt anybody."[11]

The editor of Washington D. C.'s Evening Star disagreed, exhorting the authorities and concerned citizens in a sensational headline to "Watch Him! The American Suspected of Whitechapel Butcheries Arrives in New York."[12]

New York City Police Chief Thomas F. Byrnes refused to extradite Tumblety to England. He told the press:

> There is no proof of his complicity in the Whitechapel murders. The crime for which he is under bond in London is not extraditable.[13]

In other words, since laws in both nations classified "gross indecency" as a convictable misdemeanor, rather than felony, one guilty of it could not be shipped across the Atlantic for prosecution. Byrnes knew Tumblety booked out of England to avoid the possibility of eight years' incarceration for gay "hanky-panky." In light of his deteriorating health, such a punishment would have been a death sentence.

Retreating from trouble had always been a feature of Tumblety's modus operandi. He bugged out of St. John, New Brunswick in September 1860 to escape prison time for the death of patient James Portmore, quit Washington D.C. in August 1862 after being investigated for selling phony discharge papers to soldiers, and fled Pittsburgh around December 1868 when disgruntled female patients complained to police about his insulting manner. Several more instances of his flight instinct could be mentioned. When things got too hot for peripatetic Tumblety, he beat it out of Dodge, and headed for greener pastures.

The New York World poked fun at the clumsy gumshoe Scotland Yard dispatched to locate Tumblety.

> ... A new character appeared on the scene, and it was not long before he completely absorbed the attention of everyone. He was a little man with enormous red side whiskers, ... dressed in a ... tweed suit. ... He could not be mistaken ... Everything about him told of his mission. From his ... billycock hat

... down to the bottom of his thick boots, he was a typical English detective. If he had been put on stage, ... he would have been called a caricature ... His headquarters was a saloon on the corner, where he held long conversations with the barkeeper, always ending in both of them drinking together. The (bartender) epitomized the (talks) by saying: 'He wanted to know about a feller named Tumblety, and I says I didn't know nothin' ... about him' ...[14]

Along with bum press from The New York World, were favorable articles about Tumblety in the Brooklyn Daily Eagle and New York Sun. In late January 1889 his friends at The Eagle published an embellished summary of Francis's career, along with testimonials of his sterling character from clergymen, physicians, business leaders, and politicians. In January 1889 The New York Sun asserted: "Dr. Tumblety is not what slanders say he is, but a very much abused gentlemen."[15] In the past Francis had advertised regularly with both papers. He greased editors' palms to get complimentary items printed. Long a familiar figure in their offices, Tumblety typically showed up in the role of a big shot, bearing boxes of cigars, bottles of top shelf whiskey, and cash. At that very moment the Eagle's job-printing department worked on the vanity publication of his autobiography's 1889 edition.

On December 5th Tumblety gave police the slip, hiding out at sister Elizabeth Powderly's farm in Waterloo, New York. He didn't resurface in New York City until late January when reporters spotted him at Helen Lamb's boarding house, 204 Washington St. in Brooklyn, posing as bland and faceless "Mr. Smith." Without going into the indecency charges, Tumblety informed news hounds that London police had not arrested him as a murder suspect. He explained:

I happened to be there when these Whitechapel murders attracted the attention of the whole world, and, in the company with thousands of other people I went down to the Whitechapel district. I was not dressed in a way to attract attention ... I was interested by the excitement and ... crowds and the queer scenes and sights, and did not know that all the time I was being followed by English detectives.[16]

Tumblety claimed they tailed him because he wore a slouch hat.

My guilt was very plain to the English mind. Someone had said Jack the Ripper was an American. ... It is the universal belief among the lower classes that all Americans wear slouch hats; therefore Jack the Ripper must wear (one). With the fact that I was an American was enough for the police. It established my guilt beyond question.[17]

He denied being a misogynist.

I will show you one little evidence that I am not regarded with aversion by the (feminine) sex. ... I had received a letter of introduction to a lady of rank, a duchess, who was then at Torquay which is several hundred miles from London. I presented my letter and was invited to breakfast ... When I came I (gave) her a bouquet of flowers, and she picked up a quill ... and dashed off the following stanzas extempore:

'To Dr. Francis Tumblety, M.Ed:
Thanks for lovely rosebud scent,
Its beauty may be fleeting,
But not its sentiment,
And its charming beauty,
Nor color cannot last,

It will be a pleasant duty
In memory of the past
To guard the faded flower,
When you have gone from me,
In memory of the hour
You came to sweet Torquay.
    Mary.'[18]

In spite of such folderol, the weight of anecdotal evidence proved his misogyny. In 1875 The Liverpool Leader newspaper recorded this instance of his rude treatment of a female patient.

> There comes to us a tale of a decent woman from the Isle of
> Man who sought his advice respecting a bad leg. He told her it
> was due to the immorality of her parents, but would cure it for
> 3 pounds. This she declined, whereon he ordered her to get
> out, legs and all, or else he would kick her out! Other women
> young and unmarried have fled in alarm from his premises,
> and say his language and conduct suggested danger.[19]

Buffalo acquaintance C. A. Bloom recalled a chance meeting with Tumblety during the time of the Ripper murders.

> One pleasant day in October (1888) in company with my
> wife and another lady, I was going down Regent St. (in an
> omnibus) ... I was surprised to see ... Dr. Tumblety enter (it)
> at Oxford St. But what surprised me were his actions when he
> found I was (with) the ladies. When I introduced my wife to
> him his (behavior was) so strange that she has spoken about
> it several times since ... He seemed very ill at ease and never
> raised his eyes from the floor.[20]

When in Rochester during the spring of 1885, Francis snubbed 33 year old Eleanor McMullin while visiting her paralyzed mother Eveline, who'd been a good friend of his late mother Margaret. On May 8, 1905 a lawyer for Tumblety's relatives deposed Eleanor. Michael Hawley summarized her testimony as follows:

> (Tumblety) did not pay the slightest attention to her. She felt the failure to observe her was discourteous because she was the oldest daughter and woman of the house. She told the attorney that she was dressed in a manner as would have attracted ... any man. The lack of attention by Tumblety was significant enough to have the whole family discuss this afterward.[21]

That incident deserves consideration because of what it reveals about Tumblety. He showed respect for disabled matriarch Eveline McMullin, while shunning her attractive daughter. Tumblety accepted maternal women as breeders and nurturers, but detested those he perceived as seductive tarts who led men astray.

In 1869 Tumblety tried to hire bellboy James D. Maguire, who worked at St. Louis's Southern Hotel as his valet. Twenty years later Maguire confirmed Tumblety's misogyny, adding that "his antipathy to fallen women has been especially marked."[22]

Tumblety could not endure being in the presence of stylish women. Baltimore attorney Frank M. Widner Jr. recalled him in the waiting room of his office, "holding a newspaper in front of his face when women walked by."[23] Once a nice-looking lady inadvertently erred by sitting next to him. "He threatened (her) so much that she left the room."[24] Tumblety likened pretty young females to ancient Greek sirens with centerfold looks and beautiful singing voices, who enticed sailors to their destruction.

In short, Tumblety's anti-female tirades and actions were so abundant that a whole volume of sentimental odes to him by the Duchess of Torquay couldn't explain them away.

Because Scotland Yard profiled Jack the Ripper as a medical maniac, it issued an order to bring all quacks into headquarters for interrogation. Thus, unconventional medicine man Tumblety tumbled into their dragnet. When reviewing his file English investigators would not only have seen past morals charges, but instances of fraud, malpractice, and Irish Home Rule agitation.

On the evening of June 4, 1889, while still under suspicion for the Whitechapel murders, Tumblety sauntered through Manhattan's Washington Square, and solicited a young man named George Davis for sex. Davis spurned his advances and called him "a base name," whereupon Tumblety struck him repeatedly on the face and neck with his cane. Police arrived and hauled both men to Mercer St. station. At a hearing before Judge Ford on June 25th Francis pled not guilty. An assistant district attorney declined to prosecute him because he judged Davis "untruthful and shiftless."[25]

Back in the Lineup 105 Years Later

Interest in Francis Tumblety as a Ripper suspect revived in 1993 after retired Suffolk police officer Stewart P. Evans discovered a letter written in 1913 by London Chief Inspector John G. Littlechild to journalist George R. Sims. 1913 marked the 25th anniversary of the Whitechapel murders. Sims asked if the Metropolitan Police had formed any new theories about the Ripper's identity. Littlechild wrote: "Amongst the suspects, and to my mind a very likely one, was a doctor, an American quack named Tumblety."[26]

Scotland Yard profiled Jack the Ripper as a middle-class night prowler who seemed drawn to Whitechapel's slums. In the estimation of Hot Springs hotel proprietor A. R. Smith, Tumblety fit that description. "You would always find him on the streets ... at night."[27] Dr. John Brooks of Hot Springs testified that Tumblety associated with "the worst-looking tramps he could pick up, ... regular hobos. ... He would always take the dark side of the street, where there were no lights."[28] One night around 1895 former Rochester neighbor Eleanor McMullin saw Tumblety hiding in a dark alley.

> I was going down town Saturday evening, and on the right hand side of Main St. as I passed the doorway I saw (Tumblety); he was tight against the wall as he could be, with his hands down at his side, looking furtively out.[29]

Richard Norris corroborated those impressions.

> It seems to me he had peculiar habits, every night going through dark streets, walking like a street walker.[30]

Philo Smith, part owner of St. Louis's Mona House, also confirmed his nocturnal bent. "Dr. Tumblety kept to his room most all the day time; night time he was around (town)."[31]

However, police knew Tumblety to be a homosexual, thus not a likely patron of female prostitutes. London Metropolitan Police and Scotland Yard lost interest in him after the brutal murder of Alice McKenzie on July 17, 1889. The perpetrator cut 40 year old Alice's throat and mutilated her "lower abdomen." Detectives and forensic pathologists were divided as to whether or not Jack the Ripper committed that atrocity. Dr. George Bagster Phillips concluded that the killer must have been left-handed, whereas Jack was certainly right-handed. His colleague Dr. Thomas Bond believed this heinous crime to be the Ripper's work. Assistant Police Commissioner Sir Robert Anderson sided with Phillips. Chief Inspector James Monro agreed with Dr. Bond that, regardless of right or left-handedness, both m.o. and offender signature pointed to "Jack" as the culprit. In any event, Alice McKenzie's murder took the heat off Tumblety.

Endnotes

1 London Evening Post, February 16, 1889.

2 Cincinnati Enquirer, December 14, 1888.

3 Michael L. Hawley, Jack the Ripper Suspect Dr. Francis Tumblety, Sunbury Press, Mechanicsburg, PA p. 6 op. cit. George R. Sims, Sunday Referee, 1907.

4 Chicago Tribune, October 7, 1888.

5 London Evening News, October 18, 1888.

6 Timothy B. Riordan, Prince of Quacks, McFarland & Co., Inc., Jefferson, NC, 2009, p. 177.

7 Hawley, p. 162. Tumblety's motto used in advertisements and various editions of his autobiographies, which he took from herbalist Samuel Thomson's poem "Lobelia Speakers for Itself," published in The Thomsonian Recorder, June 6, 1835.

8 Ibid., p. 22, op. cit. September 23, 1913 letter of John G. Littlechild to George R. Sims.

9 Ibid., p. 223.

10 New York World, December 4, 1888.

11 New York Herald, December 4, 1888.

12 Neil R. Storey, The Dracula Secrets, The History Press, Stroud, Gloucestershire, 2012, p. 230, op. cit. The Evening Star, December 3, 1888.

13 New York Sun, December 4, 1888.

14 Ibid.

15 New York Sun, January 29, 1889.

16 New York World, January 29, 1889.

17 Ibid.

18 Ibid.

19 Liverpool Leader, January 9, 1875.

20 Buffalo Courier, December 7, 1888.

21 Hawley, 180-181.

22 Hawley, p. 73, op. cit. The St. Louis Republic, January 17, 1889.

23 Estate of Francis Tumblety Probate Proceedings, Statement of Frank M. Widner, Jr., Esq.

24 Ibid.

25 New York Times, August 10, 1889.

26 Hawley, p. 22, op cit. September 23, 1913 letter of John G. Littlechild to George R. Sims.

27 Tumblety Probate Proceedings, City of St. Louis Archives, Statement of A. R. Smith.

28 Ibid., Statement of Dr. John Brooks.

29 Ibid., May 8, 1905 Statement of Eleanor M. Elsheimer.

30 Ibid., May 12, 1905 Statement of Richard S. Norris.

31 Ibid., Statement of Philo Smith.

CHAPTER 6:

Jack the Ripper

Among the multitudinous Ripper suspects are career criminal Michael Ostrog, Polish barber Severin Klosowski, lawyer/schoolteacher Montague John Druitt, Royal Physician Sir William Gull, demented hairdresser Aaron Kosminski, Prince of Wales Albert Victor, wife beater Hyam Hyams, expressionist painter Walter Sickert, "Dr." Francis Tumblety, and dozens more—including the extremely unlikely Charles Lutwidge Dodgson (aka Lewis Carroll,) author of the children's classic Alice's Adventures in Wonderland.

Let's first list eight murders which have been imputed to Jack the Ripper, along with names of victims, their approximate ages, dates of occurrence, and likelihood of being slain by "Jack."

Martha Tabram, August 7, 1888, 39 years old, possibly killed by the Ripper

Mary Ann "Polly" Nichols, August 31, 1888, 43, murdered by the Ripper

Elizabeth Ann "Annie" Chapman, September 8, 1888, 48, Ripper victim

Elizabeth "Long Liz" Stride, September 30, 1888, 42, probable Ripper victim

Catherine "Kate" Eddowes, September 30, 1888, 46, Ripper victim

Mary Jane Kelly, November 9, 1888, 25, Ripper victim

Alice McKenzie, July 17, 1889, 39, uncertain

Frances Coles, February 13, 1891, 29, most likely not murdered by "Jack"

The senseless Whitechapel slayings shocked Victorian England. The savagery of them anticipated modern day serial killers, mass-murdering dictators, unprecedented civilian carnage caused by high-tech weaponry, and contemporary media's atheistic naturalism which depicts humans as clever-but-soulless beasts.

The five "canonical" Ripper slayings—almost certainly committed by "Jack"—were those of Polly Nichols, Annie Chapman, Elizabeth Stride, Catherine Eddowes, and Mary Jane Kelly. All those homicides took place in London's disreputable Whitechapel section during the wee hours of weekend mornings. Though slightly less than a square mile, Whitechapel contained 62 brothels and an estimated 1,200 prostitutes. The perpetrator viciously slashed victims' throats with a long knife, then maimed their bodies. Except for 25 year old Mary Jane Kelly, and possibly Elizabeth Stride, those unfortunates were impoverished alcoholic women in their forties, rather than whores.

A biographical sketch of Catherine Eddowes (1842-1888) will provide an example. She was born in Wolverington (West Midlands) on April 14, 1842, the sixth child of tinsmith George Eddowes' and his wife Catherine's eleven children.

Artist's drawing of Catherine Eddowes from the Penny
illustrated Paper, October 13, 1888.

The Eddowes family moved to London during Kate's infancy. She
and some of her siblings attended Dowgate School, where they learned to
read, write, and reckon. Unfortunately, mother Catherine Evans Eddowes
died of consumption at the age of forty on November 17, 1855 when Kate
was thirteen. George Eddowes followed his wife in death two years later.

Having a "jolly" personality, Kate preferred staying out late with the
"wrong crowd" to performing housework. Her older sister Harriet wrote
to Uncle William Eddowes in Wolverhampton and asked if he could find a
position for Kate there. He agreed to help, and arranged with his employer,
Old Hall (tinning & japanning) Works to hire her as a metal plate stamper
and tray polisher. This firm manufactured tin kettles, cups, pans, trays, and
the like. After two years of 6 AM to 6 PM drudgery at Old Hall Works 6

days per week, Kate got fired for stealing. That petty crime deeply embarrassed her uncle, leading to her expulsion from his household.

With her meager savings, Kate set off for Birmingham. At first she lived with the family of Uncle Tom Eddowes, a bareknuckle prizefighter and cobbler. She soon met Royal Irish Guards army veteran Thomas Conway (1836-1908) who supplemented his modest government pension by working as a songwriter and peddler. Uncle Tom Eddowes and his wife Rosannah did not approve of Conway, and ordered their niece to either break up with him or leave their home. She opted for the latter alternative, and ran off with Conway some time in 1861. As a token of her early infatuation with Tom, Kate had his initials tattooed on her left forearm. Though never married, the couple produced three children who survived infancy: Annie (born 1863), Thomas (1868), and George (1873).

Catherine Eddowes was 5 feet tall, with auburn hair, hazel eyes, and pleasant facial features. (Needless to say, the hideous autopsy photos of this poor woman do her no justice). Friends described her as intelligent and generous. She had a wry sense of humor and love of music, along with a volatile temper.

Tom and Kate pursued a bohemian lifestyle. During their honeymoon period the lovers roamed through England's picturesque country towns selling ballads and trinkets. A hundred years later they might have started a rock group. One of Tom's ballads has survived, "On the Awful Execution of Charles Christopher Robinson" (who happened to be a distant cousin of Kate). On August 26, 1866 this young man was executed in Wolverhampton for murdering his girlfriend Harriet Seager. Tom and Kate showed up for his hanging, sang their song, and sold copies of its lyrics.

Come all you feeling Christians,
Give ear unto my tale,
It's for a cruel murder
I was hung at Stafford Gaol.
The horrid crime that I have done
Is shocking for to hear,
I murdered one I once did love,
Harriet Seagar dear.

Charles Robinson is my name,
With sorrow was oppressed,
The very thought of what I've done,
Deprived me of my rest:
Within the walls of Stafford Gaol,
In bitter grief did cry,
And every moment seemed to say
'Poor soul prepare to die!'...

May my end a warning be
Unto all mankind,
Think on my unhappy fate
And hear me in your mind.
Whether you be rich or poor
Your friends and sweethearts love,
And God will crown your fleeting days,
With blessings from above.[1]

The complementary talents of Tom and Kate went into that ballad's composition. Since musical Tom was illiterate, Kate must have written those poetical lyrics.

At this point in their lives the romantic pair were free spirits who didn't mind roughing it. But after the birth of second child Thomas in 1868 they decided to adopt a more settled mode of living, and relocated from wild country to a small rented house at 13 Cottage Street in London.

To support his growing family, Tom took a hod carrier's job, which required travel. Despite privations the couple faced in London, their three children were educated at the highly-regarded Sutton Industrial School.

By 1870 Tom and Kate quarreled more frequently due to his long absences, her increased alcohol consumption, and their poverty. Smart and "fresh-mouthed" Kate had the lawyer's gift for debating effectively, which won most heated arguments, but further antagonized Tom. A sore loser, he resorted to fisticuffs. Kate's sisters and friends could not help noticing her blackened eyes and facial bruises. Reminiscent of their ballad about Charles Christopher Robinson, Tom once growled: "I shall be hung for you one of these days."[2] Their predicament was the reverse of most warring couples in that she drank immoderately, whereas he was an obnoxious teetotaler.

For lack of funds Kate found herself and the children in workhouses for much of 1877. In February of that year she lost infant Frederick, apparently due to a combination of stress, malnutrition, and alcoholism.

During this period she tried the patience of sisters Harriet, Elizabeth, Emma, and Eliza, all of whom had their own problems, yet sheltered her at one time or another from Conway's battering. In the end all of them dropped Kate because of her boozing, erratic behavior, and habit of bumming money.

By age fifteen daughter Annie began to keep house, cook, and look after her younger brothers, enabling Kate to earn money by cleaning houses for Jewish families in the Whitechapel area. Unfortunately, she squandered most of her income on drink.

London coppers arrested Kate frequently for public drunkenness and disorderly conduct. During those unpleasant episodes she would resist and curse at both police officers and gawkers. Magistrates typically sentenced Kate to a week or two in Wandsworth Prison, which permitted her to bring the kids along. However, she ditched sons Thomas and George for six days while on a bender in October 1879. Police took them to a workhouse. Older sister Annie had to retrieve them.

The 1881 census showed Tom and Kate still living together at 71 Lower George St. in London with their three children. Tom no longer spent much time there. Kate left that same year, effectively abandoning 13 year old Thomas and eight year old George.

Although there was plenty of guilt to go around, Kate's sisters and daughter Annie blamed her for the family's break-up. According to Victorian mores, men reigned supreme. Respectable (i.e., submissive) women must never allow themselves to degenerate into drunken and insubordinate shrews.

Conway seemed to support sons Thomas and George until they reached "adulthood" at age sixteen. At the same time, he protected his army pension against claims from Kate by legally changing his last name to "Quinn."

To escape from her dysfunctional family, Annie Conway (1863-1943) moved to London's Bermondsey Parish in 1882 with boyfriend Louis Philips, who worked as a lampblack packer. (They would marry on August 3, 1885 after she became pregnant with their third child.) To Annie's chagrin Kate found out where she lived and began showing up inebriated at her door, begging for money. In order to avoid such embarrassing scenes Annie moved without informing Kate of her new residence.

Following the birth of third child William in 1886, Annie wished to reconcile with her mother as well as recover from that difficult birth. She contacted Kate and asked if she would help her with housekeeping and babysitting tasks. Kate consented, but only on the condition that she be paid. Though taken aback by that requirement, Annie agreed to her terms. After receiving a cash deposit from Annie, Kate hit the pubs, and failed to appear for the agreed-upon care of her grandchildren, thus terminating their relationship.[3]

Sometime in 1882 Kate met fellow tippler John Kelly, an impecunious produce market porter who became her second common law husband. The couple frequented Three Bells Pub, but had no regular address. Kate and John were among the 8,500 homeless East Enders who scraped up four pence per night to sleep in one of its 223 flophouses. When broke, they'd "crash" in an abandoned shed at 24 Dorset St. which housed a scarier assortment of derelicts.

Was Kate a prostitute? Victorian society assumed that any woman out and about between 10 PM and 6 AM must be a whore. In fact, many of them were destitute alcoholics. Family members and friends acknowledged that Kate had children out of wedlock, but denied she ever worked in the sex trade. Frederick W. Wilkinson, manager of Cooney's Lodging House, who'd known her for seven years, testified that he "never knew or heard of her being intimate with anyone but Kelly."[4] John Kelly himself asserted that she did not go "out for immoral purposes at night (and) never brought me money in the morning after being out."[5] Kelly added that he would not have stayed with her if she'd been sleeping around.

Every August since 1883 Kate Eddowes and John Kelly walked the 44 miles from London to Hunton (near Maidstone) for the hop harvest. In August 1888 their friend Emily Burrell accompanied them. The trek through Kentish countryside brought back memories of her of wanderings with Tom Conway in the 1860s. During "hopping" expeditions they were fed, paid 2 pence per bushel of hops, and supplied with barrels of beer and hard cider. They usually had to sleep in barns or under the stars. The migrant laborers enjoyed singing around campfires with fellow hop pickers. While taking shelter from a rain shower during their long hike back to London, Kate allegedly told Emily Burrell she knew the Whitechapel fiend's identity, and intended to collect reward money for his capture.

Could Francis Tumblety Have Been the Ripper?

In his biography of Francis Tumblety, Michael Hawley utilized estate records to build upon evidence adduced by Stewart Evans, Paul Gainey, and others which implicated him as a Ripper suspect. He quoted Richard Norris's testimony that Tumblety once opened his trunk in New Orleans and showed him a tray with "all sorts of large knives ... (and) surgical instruments."[6]

Remember that Tumblety, an apostle of naturopath Samuel Thomson, repudiated surgery, and denounced the scalpel as causing more damage than it rectified. Poseur Tumblety, always obsessed with uniforms and social rank, postured as a "multi-talented" physician in order to gain a regimental surgeon's appointment in the Union Army. He craved prestige, but not such onerous responsibilities as amputating gangrenous limbs from seriously wounded troops.

According to Michael Hawley, Tumblety's declining physical condition since 1880 motivated him to prioritize "health over money."[7] Ardent theater buff Francis spoke of belonging to The Sublime Society of Beefsteaks, which included such members as Henry Irving, Edwin Booth, Richard Mansfield, and Dracula author Bram Stoker (then Hall Caine's best friend and literary agent). Tumblety had undoubtedly seen Richard Mansfield's stage adaption of Dr. Jekyll and Mr. Hyde, produced by Stoker, with Henry Irving playing the lead role. This drama portrayed Dr. Jekyll attempting to develop an elixir of life from human body parts and fluids. At that time Tumblety himself was searching for a magic potion to heal his syphilis, heart disease, and nephritis.

One might think that an unhealthy man approaching sixty would have less libido and more common sense. Tumblety's inane friskiness while unwell seems inexplicable and irrational unless we plug in the missing puzzle piece of Reichenbach's Odic Theory. Baron Karl Ludwig von Reichenbach (1788-1869) was not simply a moony guru, but an authentic scientist who developed novel coal tar compounds such as creosote, waxy paraffin, the antiseptic phenol, picamar perfume base, and synthetic dyes. Though his Theory of Odic Force smacks of quackery, it became a popular sensation during the mid-to-late 19th Century. Newspaper addict Tumblety would have been familiar with this notion, which postulated that all plants, animals, and humans radiated "bio-magnetic" Odic energy from their soul-connected auras and chakras. Healthy children and adolescents possessed a surplus of this vital power. However, the old and sick lacked "Ods" and needed to absorb them, vampire-like, from the youthful and fit in order to survive.

Madame Helena P. Blavatsky, a proponent of Odic energy (or "prana) cited the example of Old Testament Kind David "who reinforced his failing vigor with the healthy magnetism of beautiful young maiden Abishag. "[8] Another fan of Reichenbach, Adolf Hitler, gave an example of the (usually unconscious) "vampirism" of the unfit: "...a baby cries and resists when his grandmother wants to keep hugging him; he doesn't want to pass his powers to a dying person."[9] (Hitler cited Reichenbach's theory to justify his program to euthanize the elderly and physically disabled.)

So Tumblety not only enjoyed sex with young males, he rationalized it as being therapeutic.

Advocates for Tumblety as a Ripper suspect point out how he matched that profile in certain respects. He lived in London during the Whitechapel murders, detested fallen women, possessed medical knowledge, owned a complete set of surgical instruments, collected specimens of preserved female sex organs, and sought stem-cell type remedies for his multifarious ailments. Tumblety partisans also contend that the Ripper murders stopped by the time of his arrest for homosexual acts. But that might have been due to coincidence. Metropolitan Police evidently thought so, since they shifted their interest to another man.

Hellish Correspondence

British police still wanted to interrogate Tumblety. He had a long rap sheet, employed aliases, sneaked around after dark, seemed attracted to Whitechapel's slums, possessed anatomical knowledge, had enough money to travel extensively, and reviled flirtatious women. Furthermore, he might have written at least one of the Ripper letters.

Sanford Conover (alias Colonel Charles A. Dunham) alleged that practical joker Francis Tumblety amused himself in the 1860s by "sending anonymous letters to the federal authorities...His object ... was notoriety."[10] Journalist Fred Hart related a story about Tumblety's early days in Manhattan, circa 1858, when a druggist named George Giles enraged him. He paid one of Hart's acquaintances, the stepson of a Presbyterian minister, to compose "a filthy string of verses on Giles, ... had the doggerel printed and sent ... to every house in the Ninth Ward."[11] We have already seen Tumblety's venomous letter to Hall Caine excoriating Liverpool Leader newspaper editor Richardson as a minion of Satan.

During the Whitechapel atrocities pranksters purporting to be the Ripper mailed dozens of spiteful letters to police and newspapers. Three stand out as possibly being genuine, specifically the September 25,

1888 "Dear Boss" letter, "Saucy Jacky" postcard of October 1, 1888, and "From Hell Letter," received by a Whitechapel town watch organization on October 16th. The first two were mailed to Central News Agency of London, not the police. The "From Hell" missive was posted to the home of George A. Lusk, a local contractor and Chairman of the Whitechapel Vigilance Committee.

The "Dear Boss" letter stated:

Dear Boss,

I keep on hearing the police have caught me but they won't fix me just yet. I have laughed when they look so clever and talk about being on the right track. That joke about Leather Apron gave me real fits. I am down on whores and I shant quit ripping them till I do get buckled. Grand work the last job was. I gave the lady no time to squeal. How can they catch me now. I love my work and want to start again. You will soon hear of me with my funny little games. I saved some of the proper red stuff in a ginger beer bottle over the last job to write with but it went thick like glue and I can't use it. Red ink is fit enough I hope ha. ha.

The next job I do I shall clip the lady's ears off and send to the police officers just for jolly wouldn't you. Keep this letter back till I do a bit more work, then give it out straight. My knife's so nice and sharp I want to get to work right away if get a chance. Good luck.

Yours Truly Jack the Ripper.

Don't mind me giving the trade name.

PS Wasn't good enough to post this before I got all the red ink off my hands curse it. No luck yet. They say I'm a doctor now. ha. ha.[12]

In handwriting identical to the "Dear Boss" letter, the "Saucy Jacky" postcard stated:

I was not codding dear old Boss when I gave you the tip, you'll hear about Saucy Jacky's work tomorrow double event this time number one squealed a bit couldn't finish straight off. Had not time to get ears off for police thanks for keeping letter back till I got to work again.

Jack the Ripper.[13]

Note: The "Saucy Jacky" card bore an October 1st postmark, and referred to the Stride and Eddowes murders which occurred the night before (September 30th). All of London's newspapers headlined that story. So the writer simply gathered information about those crimes from one of the morning papers, then instantly dashed off his nasty postcard, and deposited it in the nearest mailbox. (Coincidentally, Metropolitan police arrested Tumblety that day for committing "unnatural offences.")

Newspaper columnist George Sims found it odd that anyone would send correspondence to London's Central News office, which operated as a wire service, rather than newspaper. He thought that act ...

on Jack's part betrays an inner knowledge of the newspaper world ... Everything therefore points to the fact that the (jester) is professionally connected with the press.[14]

Assistant Metropolitan Police Commissioner Robert Anderson also suspected a rogue newspaper copywriter of confecting both the "Dear Boss" and "Saucy Jacky" messages.

> At that time ... sensation-mongers of the ... press fostered the belief that ... London was no longer safe... One enterprising journalist went so far as to impersonate the cause of all this terror as 'Jack the Ripper,' a name by which he will probably go down to history.[15]

Evidence pointed to hard-drinking Central News Agency copy editor Thomas J. Bulling (1847-1934). But if guilty of writing those repulsive notes, he did not face criminal charges, or termination of his employment. Central News did not sack Bulling until late July 1898 when he injudiciously reported the death of retired German Chancellor Otto von Bismarck under the header, "Bloody Bismarck Is Dead!" At that time Bulling had been depressed because of 36 year old wife Leonora's untimely death one month earlier. The 1901 census showed him living alone in a London boarding house and working as a newspaper reporter, a few rungs down from his former Central News job title as "manager, telegraphic news agency."

On October 16, 1888 around 5 PM the postal service delivered a small box wrapped in brown paper to Mr. George A. Lusk's residence at 1 Alderney Road, East London. He opened the package, which contained a crank letter and half-kidney cut longitudinally. Lusk initially assumed this outrage to be a perverse joke. The next day he showed the box and its malodorous enclosure to fellow Mile End Vigilance committee members. They took the matter more seriously, and carried it to Dr. Frederick Wiles' surgery. Since Dr. Wiles was not then present, his assistant Francis S. Reed examined the kidney, and offered his opinion that it came from a human being. On October 18th Reed brought the organ for analysis to Dr. Thomas H. Openshaw, Curator of Pathology at London Hospital. Openshaw scrutinized the severed kidney through a microscope and identified it as a human left kidney which had been pickled in spirits of wine. However, a London Star article embellished his nondescript finding by stating that the body part in question was that of a woman about 45 years of age which had the "same size, shape, and color as (Catherine Eddowes') other kidney; exhibiting similar symptoms of alcoholism and Bright's Disease ..."[16] The Birmingham Post chimed in that the organ mailed to Lusk was "a 'nutmeg' kidney ... that belonged to a person who drank heavily."[17] Dr. Openshaw objected to those unwarranted assumptions. He had not determined the kidney to be that of a woman, and made no statement about it atrophying due to alcoholism.

In all likelihood reporters for the Star, and other papers which promulgated this story, also interviewed Francis Reed, who avidly believed the half kidney mailed to Lusk was the same one "Jack" excised from Kate Eddowes' body on September 30, 1888.

London Medical Officer Dr. Sedgwick Saunders, who observed Dr. Frederick Gordon Brown's autopsy of Catherine Eddowes, supported Openshaw's scientific caution rather than the press's desire for a sensational story. To a reporter for The London Echo, he declared:

> It is a pity some people have not the courage to say they don't know. You may take it there is no difference between the male and female kidney. As for those in animals, they are similar... I think it would be quite possible to mistake it for a pig's.
>
> ... The right kidney of the woman Eddowes was perfectly normal in its structure and healthy, and by parity of reasoning,

you would not get much disease in the left. The liver was healthy and gave no indication that the woman drank...[18]

Dr. Sedgwick assumed that a malicious practical joker had mailed the kidney to George Lusk. With regard to the "discovery of the half ... kidney, and supposing it to be human, my opinion is that it was a ... prank. It is quite possible for any (medical) student to obtain a kidney for (that) purpose."[19]

In fact, Kate Eddowes did hit the bottle frequently and hard. At 8:30 PM on September 29, 1888 Police Constable Lewis Robinson saw her intoxicated and "slumped on the footpath in front of 29 Aldgate High St."[20] He and PC George Simmons escorted her to nearby Bishopgate Station jail so she could sleep it off. When Robinson asked for her name, Kate replied "nothing."

After waking up around 12:30 AM (September 30th), Catherine told turnkey George H. Hutt she'd sobered up and asked to be released. He looked her over and agreed to set her free if she would give him her name and address. Kate obliged, stating her name and usual sleeping quarters at 35 Flower St., the location of Cooney's doss house. Jailer Hutt unlocked her cell about 1 AM and asked her to shut the station door on her way out. As she walked past Hutt, insolent Kate said: "All right, good night, old cock,"[21] then flung open Bishopgate's main door and moseyed out without bothering to close it.

Forty-five minutes later PC Edward Watkins discovered her mutilated corpse laying on the southwest corner of Mitre Square.

Francis Reed brought the "From Hell" letter and piece of kidney from Dr. Openshaw's office to Scotland Yard's Leman Station for safekeeping. Most cops agreed with George Lusk and Dr. Saunders that the letter and organ had been sent by a depraved prankster, and was not necessarily the mate of Ms. Eddowes' other kidney.

Both the original "From Hell Letter" and half kidney delivered by Reed disappeared long ago. A considerable portion of Metropolitan Police files on the Whitechapel murders have been lost due to fires, Luftwaffe bombing raids during World War II, and shoddy record-keeping. To fill in the blanks, scholars rely on newspaper archives, public records, and the memoirs of Assistant Metropolitan Police Commissioner Robert Anderson, Assistant C.I.D. Chief Constable Melville L. Machnachten, and Police Commissioner Charles Warren.

The "From Hell Letter's" misspellings, crabbed syntax, and lack of punctuation suggest that it was scrawled by a barely literate foreigner.

From Hell

Mr Lusk

Sor

I send you half the kidne I took from one women prasarved it for you tother piece I fried and ate it was very nise I may send you the bloody knif that took it out if you only wate a whil longer

Signed

Catch me when you can

Mishter Lusk.[22]

On October 20, 1888, The London Evening News published a provocative story police heard from Miss Emily Marsh, who worked the counter in her father's leather goods shop. Shortly after 1 PM on October 15, 1888, a stranger dressed like a priest entered the store and asked her if she knew Mr. George Lusk's address. She said patrons of the nearby Crown Pub could tell him, or his Mile End Vigilance Committee colleague Joseph Aarons, who lived on Jubilee St. The priest replied that he didn't want to go into a pub, or bother Mr. Aarons. Emily then consulted a recent newspaper which contained an article about Mr. Lusk. It mentioned that he lived on Alderney Road, but did not give his house number. Her visitor wrote down that street name, thanked her, and left. (The "From Hell Letter" was addressed to Alderney Road, without a house number). Miss Marsh described him as 45 years old, 6 feet in height, with an Irish accent, and mustache. Shop boy John McCormack confirmed her description. This sounds like someone familiar to us: "Father" Francis Tumblety.

Pittsburgh grapho-analyst Michelle Dresbold examined the handwriting on the "From Hell Letter" and ascertained that it matched Tumbletey's penmanship, based on his distinctive capital "I's," as well as the long, descending loops on lower case cursive "f"s," "g's," "p's," and "y's."

Perceptive readers detected Irish expressions in the text, such as "prasarved," "tother," and "nise."

As to the kidney enclosed, anatomical specimen collector Tumblety always seemed to have a body parts connection. His source in London might have been the young American doctor with whom he exchanged prurient letters.

Assistant Police Commissioner Robert Anderson took action after receiving the "From Hell Letter." He cabled San Francisco Police Chief Patrick Crowley on October 29th, 1888, and asked him for samples of Tumblety's handwriting, which could be obtained from that city's Hibernia Savings & Loan Association. Crowley acquired the requested files from

Hibernia executive Charles F. Smythe, had them photographed, then sent the photos via diplomatic post to Anderson in mid-November. Scotland Yard's efforts to shadow and interrogate Tumblety suggest that its graphologists must have judged his penmanship similar to the "From Hell" letter. (London police already had Tumbley's salacious correspondence addressed to boyfriends, but preferred to have writing specimens on legal documents which were witnessed and notarized.)

If Tumblety wrote the "From Hell Letter," he did so simply to taunt the cops. London's Metropolitan Police had charged him with four indecent assaults against young males. We can only guess that he couldn't resist an opportunity to make his perennial antagonists on the police force look like bumbling dolts.

Tumblety didn't conceal his contempt for British authorities after reaching the United States. A New York World article recorded one of his rants.

> There is no doubt left by Tumblety as to what he thought of the English police. He was emphatically scathing and abusive. 'I think their conduct in this Whitechapel affair is enough to show what they are. Why, they stuff themselves all day with pot pies and drink gallons of stale beer, keeping it up until they go to bed late at night, and then wake up the next morning heavy as lead. ... All English police have dyspepsia. They can't help it. ... Their heads are (dense) as the London fogs. You can't drive an idea through their thick skulls with a hammer. I never saw such a stupid set ...'[23]

Witness Accounts

Arguments against Tumblety's involvement in the Whitechapel homicides mention the lack of eyewitness evidence for a 58 year old, 6' 1" tall, 190 pound male with an effeminate voice and limp. His criminal record between the 1850s and 1888 consisted almost exclusively of fraud, homoerotic acts, and medical malpractice cases, rather than violent crimes. British authorities did not believe Tumblety perpetrated the murders, but thought he might know who did. They believed him temperamentally incapable of massacring women on public streets.

Having received several false sightings of "Jack," Met detectives were well aware of discrepancies in eyewitness reports. At 11 PM on September 30th, John Best and John Gardner observed Elizabeth Stride in the company of an Englishman about 5' 5" with dark mustache and sandy eyelashes; William Marshall described "Long Liz's" companion at 11:45 as middle-aged, stout, and clean-shaven. On November 8, 1888, Mary Jane Kelly's friend Mary Ann Cox saw her talking to a short, stocky man with blotchy face and carroty mustache, who wore a billycock hat, and carried a quart can of beer. This bloke turned out to be John Henry Piggott, a ship's cook with hankerings for drink, loose women, and bar fights.

However, we can discern a pattern of relatively accurate witness identifications in the Ripper case. On September 8, 1888, around 2 AM Emily Walter saw victim Annie Chapman talking to a foreigner with dark beard, about 5' 6". Elizabeth Long described him as dark-haired, "shabby-genteel," and sporting a deerstalker hat.

One of the best descriptions of "Jack" came from tobacco products salesman Joseph Lawende. At approximately 1:35 AM on September 30, 1888, after exiting the Imperial Club at 16-17 Duke St. with friends Joseph Hyam Levy and Harry Harris, he'd seen Catherine Eddowes talking with a pale-faced, mustachioed man, about 5' 7", medium build, in his 20s or early

30s, with the rough appearance of a sailor, who wore a dark serge jacket, red kerchief, grayish "salt-and-pepper" trousers, and peaked mariner's cap.

Lawende noticed that the woman held her hand on the man's chest, as if she were trying to keep him at bay. She spoke to him in the animated manner of one remonstrating with another. Friends knew Kate Eddowes to be blunt and direct. Did she recognize this guy as the Ripper, and give him a piece of her mind?

Kate probably got bad vibes from "Jack." He'd murdered Elizabeth Stride on nearby Berner St. fifty minutes earlier. The Ripper no doubt washed himself off in a horse trough, but under Mitre Square's gaslights Kate might have noticed blood spatter on his shirt collar. He stood still while she lectured him, waiting for Lawende, Hyams, and Harris to pass by. "Jack" knew that police constable Watkins, who had just walked through St. Botolph Church's passageway, wouldn't be back for a while. Shortly after the three men disappeared from sight, he struck, whipping out a razor-sharp knife at least six inches long, slitting Catherine's throat, then slicing open her body and face. City police surgeon Dr. Frederick Gordon Brown ruled her death from a severed carotid artery immediate, and the mutilations post mortem.

The Murder of Mary Jane Kelly

The Ripper definitely indulged in cosplay. His two favorite disguises were the "Jack Tar" sailor suit, and "Gentleman Jack" outfit. He donned his gent's costume on the night of November 8, 1888. Produce store owner Matt Packer sold grapes to a man accompanied by Mary Jane Kelly. This individual was twenty-five to thirty, about 5' 7" with long black coat buttoned up, soft felt "Yankee" hat, broad shoulders—rough voice, fast-talking.

Two months behind in her rent and threatened with eviction, Mary Jane worked overtime that night. Around 11:45 PM neighbor Mary Ann

Cox saw her with William Henry Piggott. Later, at 1 AM (November 9th) Ms. Cox heard her singing "Only a Violet I Plucked from my Mother's Grave." At 2 AM Ms. Kelly's ex-boyfriend George Hutchinson spotted her with a respectably-dressed man, possibly Jewish, near the intersection of Thrawl & Commercial streets. This male approached Kelly, tapped her on the shoulder, and whispered in her ear. Both laughed. She said: "All right my dear, come along. You will be comfortable."[24] He put his arm around her shoulder. Mary Jane mentioned that she'd lost her handkerchief. He gallantly pulled out a red one (just like the kerchief worn by Kate Eddowes' killer), and handed it to her. She took it and they strolled toward her apartment in Millers Court. Mary Jane's companion appeared to Hutchinson as surly, brown-eyed, with bushy eyebrows, pale face, and dark mustache turned up at the ends. He looked like a foreigner and wore a white shirt, black tie with horseshoe pin, gold watch chain hanging from his vest, long coat with astrakhan trim, and dark spats over light boots. He "walked softly," carried brown kid gloves in his right hand, and a parcel in his left.

Mary Jane Kelly might have previously met this client, since she invited him into her apartment. When discovered by police, her blood-soaked body was partially clad in a nightgown. Police deduced that "Jack" strangled her to death, then savagely disfigured her corpse.

Most experts believe the Ripper's murderous binge ended with the slaughter of Mary Jane Kelly on November 9, 1888.

Unlikely Suspect Tumblety

Francis Tumblety did not fit the description of a dark-haired, pale-faced man in his twenties, about 5'7" in height. Fifty-eight year old Tumblety stood over six feet tall, had a florid face, and ineptly dyed his graying hair and mustache with a substance similar to black shoe polish, which would dribble down his face whenever he perspired or got caught in a rain storm.

By 1888 Francis conspicuously dragged one foot behind the other as he walked.

The whole police force knew Tumblety stalked young men after sundown. But women? In his testimony during the Tumblety probate hearing, Richard S. Norris described an incident which took place in New Orleans during Mardi Gras of 1893.

> I took him to a sporting house (brothel) one night ... as a joke ... and (said) wouldn't he go in with me ... He ordered wine and a couple of girls went over to him and he said 'go away from me.' After drinking the wine he said to me. 'Let's get out of here.' We went out of the house, and he gave me a terrible lecture ...[25]

Tumblety had a lifelong aversion to sensual women. Was he the type who would seek out prostitutes on the street?

Advocates for the theory that Tumblety was Jack the Ripper have argued that psychopathic gay men do kill women for "anger-retaliatory," rather than sexual motives. While true, that's the exception, not the rule. Most homosexual and bisexual serial killers—Jeffrey Dahmer, John Wayne Gacy, William Bonin, Wayne Williams, Andrew Cunanan, etc.—murdered males. The gender of victims generally corresponds with perpetrators' sexual orientation. Thus, such heterosexual serial killers as Ted Bundy, Samuel Little, and Jack the Ripper exclusively preyed upon women.

Since veteran cops and judges develop a sixth sense when sizing up suspects, their opinions ought to be taken seriously. Seasoned police magistrate James L. Hannay would not have set low bail for Tumblety if he thought him involved with the Ripper murders. A Toronto Daily Mail reporter asked Scotland Yard Detective Walter Andrews if he knew

Tumblety. He replied: "Of course I do, but he is not the Whitechapel murderer. All the same we would like to interview him."[26] Sure of Tumblety's innocence, New York City Police Chief Thomas F. Byrnes refused to hand him over to British authorities. According to the New York World, Byrnes "laughed at the suggestion that he (Tumblety) was the Whitechapel murderer."[27] Former cop James Pryor, who worked as house detective for The Fifth Ave. Hotel, had known Francis for years. When asked by a reporter if he believed him to be Jack the Ripper, he answered, "Certainly not![28] All of those old pros pegged Tumblety as a misogynistic homosexual who spurned sexually attractive women.

Following his run-ins with law enforcement in London, Francis showed signs of physical and psychological enervation. The New York World characterized him as very anxious.

> Dr. Tumblety talked in a quick, nervous fashion, and at times … he would get up from his chair and walk rapidly around the room until he became calm …[29]

After his arrest as a suspicious person on November 17, 1890, The Washington Post depicted him as hulking, yet feeble.

> Dr. Tumblety is an enormous man, over six feet in height … His hair is black, tinged with grey, and his skin is red and coarse. His mustache is a rather large affair, evidently dyed black … His eyes are steely blue, and he gazed steadily at nothing (and) spoke in a weak, effeminate voice.[30]

Francis Tumblety's life revealed a karmic pattern of being accused of misdeeds, both rightly and wrongly. His reputation as a fraudster and pederast caused people to think him capable of any outrage. Yet he did not abduct Isaac Golladay, steal Henry Govan's wallet in New Orleans, participate in the Lincoln assassination plot, nor commit the Whitechapel murders.

Endnotes

1 Hallie Rubenhold, The Five, Houghton Mifflin Harcourt, Boston, New York, 2019, pp.223-224, op. cit. Jarrett Kobek, "May My End a Warning Be," Catherine Eddowes and Gallows Literature in the Black Country."

2 Ibid., p. 234, op. cit. Daily News, October 4, 1888.

3 All of Annie Conway Philips' children predeceased her. Sons Louis, William and Thomas were killed in World War I, which made her a triple gold star mother. By implication Catherine Eddowes posthumously became a triple gold star grandmother.

4 Ibid., p. 245, op. cit. London Metropolitan Archives, Inquest 041/191/3/65/135, Statement of Frederick William Wilkinson.

5 Ibid., Daily Telegraph, October 5, 1888.

6 Estate of Francis Tumblety Probate Proceedings, City of St. Louis, MO Archives, Statement of Richard S. Norris, May 12, 1905.

7 Michael L. Hawley, Jack the Ripper Suspect Dr. Francis Tumblety, Sunbury Press, Mechanicsburg, PA, 2018, p. 223.

8 Helena P. Blavatsky, Isis Unveiled, Michael Gomes, editor, Quest Books, Wheaton, IL, 1997, p. 52. (Cf. The Bible, 1 Kings: 1-4.)

9 Otto Wagener, Memoirs of a Confidante, Henry Ashby Turner, editor, translated by Ruth Hein, Yale University Press, New York, 1985, p. 35. Hitler used Reichenbach's dubious Theory of Odic Energy to justify his euthanasia campaign against elderly and handicapped persons by characterizing them as parasites who debilitated the young and able by sucking life force from them.

10 Rochester Democrat & Republican, December 3, 1888.

11 San Francisco Daily Examiner, November 23, 1888.

12 casebook.org, Butcher's Row Suspect, p. 11.

13 Wikipedia, "Dear Boss Letter."

14 Ibid., "Saucy Jacky Postcard."

15 Casebook.org (Robert Anderson, Criminals & Crime, J. Nisbet & Co., London, 1907).

16 Richard Jones, www.jack-the-ripper.org., p. 10 op. cit. George R. Sims article on alleged Ripper letters.

17 London Star, October 19, 1888.

18 Birmingham Post, October 19, 1888. Dr. Frederick Gordon Brown's autopsy report stated that Catherine Eddowes' remaining kidney showed signs of uremia and Bright's Disease. However, her liver appeared healthy.

19 The London Echo, October 19, 1888.

20 Ibid.

21 Wikipedia, Catherine Eddowes, op. cit. Stewart Evans & Donald Rumbelow, Jack the Ripper: Scotland Yard Investigations, Stroud, Gloucestershire, 2006, p. 115.

22 Wikipedia, "From Hell Letter." Suspect Aaron Kosminski could not have written the "From Hell Letter." He struggled with the English language, mainly spoke Yiddish, and probably could not write in Western Europe's cursive style.

23 New York World, January 29, 1889.

24 casebook.org (George Hutchinson's Statement re: Mary Jane Kelly's companion.)

25 Francis Tumblety Probate Proceedings, City of St. Louis Archives, (Statement by Richard S. Norris, May 12, 1905.)

26 Toronto World, December 12, 1888.

27 New York World, December 4, 1888.

28 Pittsburgh Chronicle & Telegraph, November 27, 1888.

29 New York World, January 29, 1889.

30 Washington Post, November 18, 1890.

CHAPTER 7:

The Enigmatic Prime Suspect

Baffling DNA Results

Russell Edwards, author of Naming Jack the Ripper (2014,) deserves credit for jump-starting research on the Whitechapel murderer. He had been interested in the Ripper murders for several years. Like many of us, Edwards eventually became frustrated by conflicting theories and the ridiculously long list of suspects. In 2007 a friend texted him that the shawl of victim Catherine Eddowes had been put up for auction. Edwards successfully bid on it. Along with the shawl he obtained a letter from its seller which explained how it came into his family's possession. This man declared that his great-grandfather, Acting Sergeant Amos Simpson of Scotland Yard, had served in the East End of London during the Ripper's killing spree. At that time no evidence kits were preserved. Police simply burned the personal effects of homicide victims. Simpson informed a superior officer that his wife was a seamstress, and asked if he could have Catherine Eddowes' silk wrap. The captain let him take it.

Unfortunately, this thoughtful surprise gift horrified Simpson's wife, who promptly tossed the bloodstained article into her rag bag. The couple's children heard about the shawl's history, and never discarded it. Neither did anyone attempt to clean the soiled thing. Two generations passed it down as a relic commemorating grandfather Amos's police service.

Sometime around 2001 a descendant of Sergeant Simpson brought the shawl to Scotland Yard's Black Museum for identification and safekeeping. The staff there viewed the stained garment as an interesting curiosity, but never exhibited it because the family's story amounted to little more than unverifiable hearsay. According to their research Amos Simpson had been stationed in Cheshunt (Hertfordshire), twenty-five miles from Whitechapel at the time of the murders. But that does not mean he could not have been temporarily transferred to London to assist with what Queen Victoria and Prime Minister Robert Cecil, Marquis of Salisbury, both perceived as a domestic crisis.

Though now smudged and mottled with holes, the shawl had once been a well-off lady's prized possession.[1] After examining this item's workmanship, dye hues, and elaborate daisy pattern, an appraiser identified it as being produced circa 1820 by Moscow's famed Pavlovsky Posad Manufactory.

What was poor Kate Eddowes doing with an heirloom Russian cape? Most Ripperologists surmised that "Jack" himself brought that article to the murder scene. Although one would think he needed to travel light, the Ripper tended to carry "parcels." He discovered from experience that silk did not function well as a towel. After Kate's grisly murder, he tossed away the fancy cloak, then cut off a piece of her cotton apron to wipe off his bloody hands and knife. (Armchair sleuths have speculated that weirdo Jack might have endowed his mother's or grandmother's cape with ritualistic significance.)

Shortly after purchasing the shawl, Russell Edwards engaged Dr. Jari Louhelainen, a lecturer in molecular biology at Liverpool's John Moores University, to analyze genetic material on it, which was believed to contain DNA from both Catherine Eddowes and her killer. After examining the garment Dr. Louhelainen established that the female victim had shed arterial blood, which would have been consistent with a person who had her throat slashed.

Edwards hired genealogists to track down descendants of Catherine Eddowes, who had a daughter and two sons by common law husband Thomas Conway. They identified Karen Miller as one of Kate's great-great granddaughters. She agreed to donate a DNA sample, which matched the mitochondrial DNA left on the shawl by Kate Eddowes.

Dr. Louhelainen put the silk wrap under infrared and ultraviolet lights to locate matter deposited by the male actor. He eventually detected squamous cells, from either skin or bodily secretions such as blood or saliva. Male DNA degrades more quickly than female (mitochondrial) DNA. Whether the man's deposits were semen, blood, sweat, or mucus, only traces of his mitochondrial (maternal) DNA would have survived after 120 years. The genetic material exuded by Eddowes' killer revealed a long line of Jewish grandmothers.

Edwards and his genealogists immediately set about the task of trying to find a living relative of Jewish suspect Aaron Kosminski. One great-grandniece, who wished to remain anonymous, agreed to provide DNA. Dr. Louhelainen determined it to be a very close match to the presumed killer's mitochondrial DNA.

In September, 2014 when Edwards released his book, Dr. Louhelainen announced that his tests had confirmed the presence of mitochondrial DNA on the shawl from Eddowes and possibly Aaron Kosminski. Noting that his paper had not been peer-reviewed, biochemists Walther Parson and Hansi Weissensteiner from Innsbruck Medical University's Institute of Legal Medicine questioned Louhelainen's findings. Kosminski's brothers, as well as nephews and cousins on his mother's side, would have had virtually the same mitochondrial DNA as him. Therefore, mt DNA can only exclude a male suspect, not positively identify one.

In 2018 scientists from the University of Leeds peer-reviewed Louhelainen's research, and found it essentially correct, but susceptible to misinterpretation by laypersons. They concluded that the male donor's DNA strikingly resembled that of Aaron Kosminski, however the murderer could have also been a relative of Kosminski's—perhaps a cousin who had almost identical matrilineal ancestry. Scientists involved in the study called this unknown man "M."

In March 2019 The Journal of Forensic Sciences published an article by Dr. Louhelainen and Dr. David Miller, a geneticist from University of Leeds. Their paper stated that:

> Mitochondrial DNA on the shawl matched the female victim's ... DNA sequence, and ... also ... the suspect candidate's mitochondrial DNA sequence. However, (there were) two differences between the (perpetrator's) mt DNA (and Kosminski's).[2]

Nevertheless, Russell Edwards remained committed to the notion that Aaron Kosminski was Jack the Ripper.

Some critics panned The Journal of Sciences' article. Turi King Ph.D. faulted it for not fully presenting genetic data, and failing to observe controlled laboratory procedures. Louhelainen and Miller used a series of dumbed-down graphs to illustrate their hypothesis, rather than revealing the actual mitochondrial DNA sequences of the two subjects. Someone on Journal of Sciences' editorial board thought publishing detailed DNA sequences violated the UK's Medical Privacy Act, but attorneys pointed out that the law did not forbid publicizing mitochondrial DNA from males because such data was not individual-specific; it applied to sundry men in the same matrilineal line.

Others strove to disqualify the shawl as hopelessly contaminated. Various individuals had fingered it, thereby tainting residues left by the 1888 donors. Ms. King cited a photograph of Russell Edwards holding the article with ungloved hands, and rumors that descendants of Catherine Eddowes and Aaron Kosminski had been in its presence. Journalist Kay Burgess wrote: "The shawl has been openly handled by loads of people, and been touched, breathed on, spat upon."[3]

Even if one concedes that many people came into contact with it, how do we account for the one in a billion chance that this piece of ladies' apparel contains well-aged mitochondrial DNA from both Kate Eddowes and a male from the Kosminski clan?

A Cursory Examination of Kosminski's Family Tree

Aaron Mordechai Kosminski was born in Klodawa, Poland (Russian Empire) on September 11, 1865 to Golda Lubnowska Kozminski and her husband, tailor Abram Kozminski. The couple's son Isaac Kosminski and his wife Bertha emigrated to London circa 1880. Isaac's sisters Mathilde and Betsy first went to Germany with their husbands, then to London during the summer of 1881. They left because of Russia's persecution of Jews, which intensified after anarchists assassinated Tsar Alexander II on March 13, 1881. Sometime in 1882 widowed mother Golda and younger brother Aaron arrived. For the next nine years those two bounced back and forth between the Whitechapel residences of Mathilde and Betsy.

By 1883 eighteen year old Aaron worked as a barber in Whitechapel. Unfortunately, he began exhibiting symptoms of paranoid schizophrenia in 1885. On July 12, 1890—two years after the Whitechapel murders—Aaron's brother-in-law Woolf Abrahams brought him to Mile End Town Workhouse for threatening Betsy Abrahams (Aaron's older sister) with a knife. The workhouse released him three days later. Police returned

Kosminski there on February 4, 1891. Because of worsening mental illness Aaron was transferred to Colney Hatch Lunatic Asylum, where he stayed for the next three years.

According to his file at Colney Hatch, Kosminski heard voices, and had a phobia about accepting food from others. He ate garbage off the street and out of trash barrels. Kosminski refused to bathe, and habitually indulged in "self-abuse," a Victorian euphemism for masturbation. In spite of his repugnant personal habits, asylum notes described him as "harmless." In April, 1892 the Metropolitan Asylums Board transferred him to Leavesden Asylum for Imbeciles near Abbots Langley, Hertfordshire. On March 24, 1919, fifty-three year old Aaron Kosminski died from a gangrenous leg. Because of his unhygienic diet he weighed only 96 pounds at the time of his death. No one visited him during his 27 year confinement at Leavesden. He was buried in London's East Ham Jewish Cemetery (Section G, Row 14, Grave #12) on March 27, 1919.

Alleged photograph of Ripper suspect Aaron Kosminski. The doe-eyed young man in this picture does not look like a homicidal maniac.

Because Kosminski was profoundly insane, most investigators have rejected him as a viable Ripper suspect."Jack" displayed extraordinary cunning which went far beyond the diminished capacities of a psychotic. He employed disguises, knew all police beats in the Whitechapel area, and deceptively put victims at ease with friendly banter, along with seemingly good-natured offers of money, food, tobacco, and alcohol.

The Invisible Man

"(Psychological data) all point to a man known to the police as 'David Cohen,' ... or someone very much like him."[4]

John E. Douglas, FBI criminal profiler

In his 1987 book The Crimes, Detection, and Death of Jack the Ripper English literature professor Martin A. Fido, Ph.D proposed Aaron Kosminski's probable relative Nathan Kaminski as the Whitechapel fiend.

"Kaminski" and "Kosminski" are both variants of the Polish surname "Kozminski," which derived from the root word "rock," and alluded to dozens of villages constructed from stone in Galicia (present day Poland and Ukraine), which were named Kamien, Kominka, etc., meaning "Rockville," "Stonetown," and the like. Nathan Kaminski (aka "David Cohen") was born in Poland the same year as Aaron Kosminski (1865).

Kaminski poses formidable challenges to genealogists. He used different names, immigrated from a foreign country, never married, owned no property, and died young. Obviously more genealogical research must be done on the Kozminski-Lubnowski-Cohen family before all dots can be connected. We're in the right ballpark, but as in life, stealthy Nathan hides in the shadows.

Ripper researchers Robert House and the late Christopher Scott uncovered interesting facts about Kaminski's background and environment. Scott found out that 15 Black Lion Yard, where he lived in the household of his "brother" (or other male relation) during the fall of 1888, had large apartments on its second story. The building's ground floor had been variously occupied as a boxing arena, oddities museum with freak show, and Yiddish theater. The British census for 1891 showed three different families residing upstairs. They were 52 year old widow Rachel Liberman and her three children in one unit; coffee shop owner Morris Morris (aka Morris Davis), in another apartment with wife Leah, son Samuel 16, Rachel Back 13, Barnett Back 8, Michael Back 6, boarders Israel Franks, collector 24, Aaron Woolf, commercial traveler 45, Sarah Salovitch, dressmaker 20, and servant Hetty Bloom 19. The third unit's household was that of 32 year old tailor Cooper Goodman, his wife Sarah 28, and their young daughters. Thus, three years after the Whitechapel murders no one with the surnames "Kaminski," "Lubnowski," or "Cohen" resided at 15 Black Lion Yard.

On England's 1881 census Christopher Scott found Black Lion Yard residents with the surnames "Abrahams" and "Cohen," but no males with the forename "Nathan."

The Kozminski family shared European Jewry's casual attitude toward last names. Since medieval times Jews would colloquially refer to "Solomon of Lubeck" or "Jacob the Shoemaker." Yet they were suspicious of goyish kingdoms' efforts to standardize surnames for purposes of better enforcing unjust taxation and political oppression. In 1782 Emperor Josef II of Austria granted civil rights to Jewish subjects under Das Toleranzpatent (Edict of Toleration), which also contained a clause requiring them to adopt permanent last names. Most compliant Jewish families stuck with the existing model by selecting monikers based on place of residence (Salzburg, Hesse, Lublin, Minsk,) occupations such as tailor

(Schneider,) glazier (Glazer,) sugar merchant (Zuckerman,) or religious tradition. "Rabinowitz" derived from "rabbi," "Cantor" from hymn singer, "Levy" from the Levite tribe, and "Cohen from "priest." Emigrating Jews frequently altered first and last names to facilitate assimilation. Hence, Polish immigrant Moishe Abramowitz would become Morris Abrams in Brooklyn.

Scott provided census enumerations for Aaron Kosminski's sisters Betsy and Mathilde. The 1891 census recorded Betsy's household as follows: Woolf Abrahams 30, 3 Sion Square, tailor, Betsy 34, (both born in Poland), Rebecca 9 (born in London), Mathilda 1.

The 1891 census for Matilde's family listed her husband Morris L. Cohen 33, 14 Greenfield St., London, boot laster, Mathilde 35, Joseph 11 (born in Germany), Bertha 9 (born in London), Annie 7, Samuel 7, Millie, 3 weeks old, and Wolf 3 weeks old.

By 1901 43 year old Morris had changed his surname to Lubnowski, his occupation to greengrocer, and address to 64 Wellsley St. Son Wolf had apparently died, but three more residents lived in his home: daughters Yetta 7, Esther 6, and mother-in-law Golda "Abrahams" 82, (actually Golda Kosminski who would die eleven years later in Tooting Bec Asylum on August 21, 1912).

Genealogist Robert House accessed Polish records to find Aaron Kosminski's birth register entry which stated a September 11, 1865 birthdate in Klodawa to parents Abram Jozef Kozminski and Golda Lubnowska. (Note: Polish surnames ending in "ski" denote a male; "ska" at the end indicates an unmarried female.)

Further digging revealed that Golda's parents were kosher butcher Walek (Wolf) Lubnowski and his wife Rudka ("Ruthie"). Two of Golda's siblings were Szymon (Simon, born 1812) and Jozek (b. 1815). Jozek and his wife Laj (Leah) produced at least four children: Rabbi Israel Simon Lubnowski Cohen (1854-1917), Morris Lubnowski Cohen (1857-1918), spouse of Aaron Kosminski's sister Mathilde, and daughters Ruchla (Rachel, b. 1859) and Gitel (b. 1866). Could Nathan Kaminski have descended from this line?

Golda Lubnowska Kozminski delivered seven children: Pessa (born 1845 who died at age 3), Hinde (b. 1850, emigrated to Massachusetts with husband Aaron Singer), Isaac (b.1851), Mathilde (b.1854), Betsy (b. 1857), Woolf (b. 1860), and Aaron (b. 1865).

Isaac apparently arrived in London first, since he was the only one enumerated on England's 1881 census. Soon thereafter he adopted wife Bertha's maiden last name "Abrahams," possibly because it sounded more English than "Kosminski." The 1881 census recorded his household as follows: Isaac Abrahams 29, tailor, 3A Fledgate St., London, wife Bertha 31, daughter Esther 6, son Mark 8, and son Woolf 2.

In 1888 Isaac lived at 179 Goulston St. in the Whitechapel district, near the residences of both younger brother Aaron and possible cousin Nathan Kaminski. As a husband and father who had a business to run, he most likely had little to do with either of these troublesome young men.

After the September 30, 1888 murders of Elizabeth Stride and Catherine Eddowes, Jack the Ripper, or someone else, wrote the "Goulston Street Graffito" on the wall of 108-119 Goulston St., a tenement complex known as the Wentworth Model buildings, on the same block as Isaac Kosminski Abrahams' apartment.

While investigating the nearby crime scene, Constable Alfred Long discovered a blood-and-feces-stained piece of cloth in the stairwell of 108-119 Goulston St. which later proved to be an exact fit with Catherine Eddowes' torn apron. On a nearby wall, Long noticed this message written in chalk: "The Juwes are the men that will not be blamed for nothing."[5] Because of its cockney mode of expression investigators assumed this ungrammatical scribbling was the work of an anti-Semitic East-Ender, who suspected an immigrant Jew of committing the recent homicides. At 5 AM, with the approval of Commissioner Charles Warren, Police Superintendent Thomas Arnold ordered patrolmen to erase the writing to prevent a possible riot against Whitechapel's Jewish population. Other detectives criticized this move because it destroyed evidence. They contended that, at the very least, a photograph should have been taken of the graffiti. In a letter to Home Undersecretary Godfrey Lushington, Warren stated that for the sake of public order he "... considered it desirable to obliterate the writing at once."[6]

Genetic Abnormalities

Like inhabitants of Ireland's rural counties, and Pennsylvania's Amish people, the inbred Ashkenazi Jews of Germany and Eastern Europe experience higher rates of mental illness than the general population. Inbreeding tends to make undesirable genetic potentials such as schizophrenia, cystic fibrosis, and Tay-Sachs Disease dominant instead of recessive.[7]

Nathan Kaminski seemed to be born with aliases. Some conjecture that his first name might actually be "Nahum" rather than "Nathan." The sparse records pertaining to him also use the names "Nathan Kaminsky" and "David Cohen." He probably emigrated to England with the extended Kozminski-Lubnowski-Cohen family in the early 1880s as an adolescent, but this has not been proven. His mother—or both parents—might have died. At some point he was apprenticed to a bootmaker. Could that have been "boot laster" Morris Lubnowski-Cohen? Nathan's residency at 15 Black Lion Yard with his brother, half-brother, brother-in-law, or uncle, reinforced the impression of him as an orphan who nobody owned. He strikes the observer as one of those grown-up waifs with psychological problems.

Street kid Nathan began consorting with prostitutes at an early age, and contracted syphilis as a teenager. As a result, he became "down on whores," and sought revenge against them. On March 24, 1888, police arrested Kaminski for a rabid public outburst, and dumped him into Stepney Workhouse. That bedlam's patient card stated his name as" Nathan Kaminsky," age 23, address 15 Black Lion Yard, occupation bootmaker, marital status single, religion Hebrew, condition syphilis, and "settlement 12 months." The latter expression meant that Nathan qualified for admittance since he'd lived in one of the East End parishes for at least a year. If we read this literally, he might not have arrived in Whitechapel until 1887. However, I believe he came to London earlier than that. Not wanting crazy Kaminski wandering the streets, Stepney Workhouse's admissions clerk simply jotted down "12 months" to indicate that he met the institution's residency requirement. A physician in Stepney's infirmary attributed Nathan's mania to venereal disease. The workhouse released him seven weeks later, on May 12th, because his symptoms seemed to subside.

Ripper scholar Chris Scott noticed a coincidence in Stepney Workhouse's records. Another inmate, 23 year old cap maker Isaac Woolfstein, who also lived at 15 Black Lion Yard, had been admitted to the infirmary on March 1, 1888 for orchitis (swollen testicles). He was still there when police brought Nathan in on March 24th. Woolfstein suffered another bout of inflamed testicles on June 4th. However, the workhouse then recorded a new address for him: 5 Gordon Place, London. Nathan and Isaac likely knew one another, and might have been related.

In the middle-to-late stages of syphilis, patients typically suffer from paresis, an inflammation of the brain which manifests as dementia. This syndrome intermittently goes into remission, causing sufferers to fluctuate between rationality and episodes of derangement. In adults over thirty it normally takes ten years for syphilis to progress into general paresis, however the disorder may effloresce more rapidly in otherwise healthy young males.

Nathan Kaminski might have shared cousin Aaron Kosminski's genetic predisposition toward paranoid schizophrenia. Thus, even minor syphilitic damage to his inner cerebrum near the amygdalae (which trigger anger, fear, and aggression) would generate flare-ups of manic behavior, marked by lack of impulse control.

Assistant Metropolitan Police Commissioner Sir Robert Anderson described Kaminski as a "sexual maniac of the most virulent type."[8] Although London Police Commissioner Sir Melville Macnaghten declared that he (i.e., Kaminski) "had a great hatred of women and strong homicidal tendencies,"[9] Macnaghten erroneously referred to him as "Kosminski" in his memoirs.

Shortly after Mary Jane Kelly's gruesome slaying in Millers Court on November 9, 1888, cockney locals in Whitechapel tipped off police about a daft bootmaker who lived in the Jewish district near that murder scene.

Met police put Kaminski under twenty-four hour surveillance. They believed family members knew about his homicidal binge, but hadn't turned him in. All Whitechapel had been abuzz about the murders for nearly three months. The killer undoubtedly returned home a bloody mess on murders dates, splattered with gore and "feculent matter."[10]

On the evening of December 5, 1888, wild-eyed Kaminski emerged from the tenement in Black Lion Yard, fulminating incoherently in Yiddish as he staggered through Whitechapel's dark alleys. According to Robert Anderson's account, the monitoring officers grabbed him, bound his hands, and transported him to Leman Station, where he spent the night in jail. The next day they brought Kaminski to Seaside House in Hove. There cigarette salesman Joseph Lawende positively identified him. Though he recognized Kaminski as the man who spoke with Catherine Eddowes minutes before her murder, Lawende refused to testify in court, and thereby become responsible for the execution of a fellow Jew at the hands of gentiles. That being the case, law enforcement officials Anderson and Macnaghten thought the best option was to keep Kaminski "caged in an asylum."[11] On December, 7th police transported him from jail to Stepney Workhouse. He was registered under the name "David Cohen" with his occupation listed as tailor rather than bootmaker. A week or so later Kaminski went berserk—hurling himself on the floor, rolling around, and shrieking epithets in both Yiddish and English. Orderlies put him in restraints and locked him into a cell.

On December 21st police transferred "Cohen" to the more secure Colney Hatch Lunatic Asylum in Barnet. That institution's file described him as having brown eyes, as well as a dark brown mustache and beard. Notes portrayed him as:

> ... spiteful and mischievous. He spat out food and had to be force fed. He tore down a lead pipe and (steel barred) window in the yard ... He was destructive, kicked passersby, and put in strong dress (i.e., a straitjacket), so as not to tear his own clothes to pieces ... In October 1889 he was confined to his bed (i.e., chained to it), and died a few days later.[12]

The England and Wales Civil Registration Death Index 1837-1915, volume 3A, page 127 showed his name as "David Cohen," and furnished the following information: age 23, from Barnet, Middlesex (location of Colney Hatch Asylum), October 20, 1888 date of demise, causes of death "exhaustion from mania (and) phthistis" (pulmonary tuberculosis). We do not have reliable information about his place of burial, however Colney Hatch had a cemetery on its property. A search on that graveyard's website yielded nothing under the names "David Cohen" or "Nathan Kaminski." However, this site collected data solely from "memorials" (i.e., headstones), a clue that Colney Hatch's interment records have been lost. In other words, pauper Nathan Kaminski's name did not appear in this burial ground's database because his grave had no tombstone.

Professor Martin Fido thought that "David Cohen" was not necessarily Nathan Kaminski's alias. In the late 19th Century British police used "David Cohen" as a generic term similar to "John Doe," when alluding to any Jewish male with an Eastern European last name.

Fido noticed that Commissioner Melville L. Macnachten, Assistant Commissioner Robert Anderson, and Chief Inspector Donald S. Swanson repeatedly mentioned "Kosminski" in their memoirs, when they actually meant Nathan Kaminski. For example, Inspector Swanson wrote these annotations in the margin of the page of Sir Robert Anderson's memoirs which certainly dealt with Kaminski (not Kosminski):

> The suspect ... was sent to Stepney Workhouse and then to Colney Hatch, and died shortly afterwards. Kosminski (sic) was the suspect.[13]

We know that Nathan Kaminski died at Colney Hatch on October 20th, 1889. Aaron Kosminski did not pass away until March 24th, 1919. Therefore, in that short passage Swanson undeniably confused Kosminski with Nathan Kaminski.

Like all louche characters, secretive Nathan took measures to creep off the grid. I could not find him on the 1881 census or London directories.

Most of the scant records on Kaminski list him under the false name "David Cohen," including his death register entry.

Shortly after the publication of Sir Robert Anderson's The Lighter Side of my Official Life in 1910, The Jewish Chronicle rebuked him for embracing the anti-Semitic "conspiracy theory" that Jack the Ripper was Jewish. A devout Presbyterian and recognized Bible scholar, Anderson had devoted 21 of his 25 books to scripture interpretation. He held the "Old Covenant" of Judaism in high esteem and therefore took umbrage at the Chronicle's unwarranted reproach. In an interview with The London Globe, Anderson asserted: "In saying he (the Ripper) was a Polish Jew, I am merely stating an ascertained fact. ... It is not a matter of theory."[14]

To sum up: on March 24, 1888 (before the Whitechapel murders) Kaminski gave his name as "Nathan Kaminsky" after being committed for psychological evaluation. But following his capture as a Ripper suspect on December 5, 1888, he refused to talk. Therefore, police officers admitted him to both Stepney Workhouse and Colney Hatch Asylum under the fictitious name "David Cohen."

Perpetual Confusion about the Ripper Case

It puzzles me why the hunt for "Jack" did not cease shortly after Nathan Kaminski's capture on December 5, 1888. Certainly there were lingering disagreements about suspects. Inspector Frederick George Abberline still leaned toward "George Chapman" (Polish barber Severin Koslowski). Sir Melville Macnachten continued to favor cricket-playing attorney-and-teacher Montague John Druitt, who ended his life that month by diving headlong from a bridge into the frigid Thames River.

Inter-service rivalry between London's Metropolitan Police and Scotland Yard led to faulty communication between those two organizations. The Whitechapel crimes happened on the Met's turf. Scotland

Yard functioned in a manner similar to our FBI, acting as a federal law enforcement agency which pursued criminals fleeing across county and state lines. London police appreciated Scotland Yard's back-up and superior forensic science resources, but did not relish the Yard's occasional reports to higher-ups which criticized its own performance.

The English public, and its law enforcement agencies, were denied closure in the Ripper case. The resolution brought by trial and hanging never occurred. Metropolitan Police surreptitiously clapped Kaminski into a madhouse, where he died in obscurity ten months later.

Combining Dr. Jari Louhelainen's DNA research with Martin Fido's deduction that "David Cohen" and Nathan Kaminski were one and the same person has not established Kaminski's guilt beyond all doubt.

Are there ways forward through this morass? Following Robert House's lead, professional genealogists in Poland should be engaged to check Polish birth records for a male child named Nathan or Nahum, born in 1865, under the surnames "Kaminski," "Lubnowski," and their variants.

More could surely be done with the perpetrator's DNA sample. DNA phenotyping service Parabon NanoLabs in Reston Virginia has developed protocols for identifying criminals by means of genetic genealogy. Since 2016 this company has solved 109 out of 500 cold cases, including the Golden State Killer mystery. In order to determine "Jack's" origin, Parabon would submit his DNA profile to online genealogical services 23andMe, GEDmatch, FamilyTreeDNA, etc. It also has the technology to create a DNA Snapshot, or sketch of the subject's face which takes into account features such as skin, hair, and eye color, face shape, freckling, bone structure, and other factors. Those methods will bring us closer to cracking "the mother of all cold cases."

There almost seems to be a secret desire—if not a vested interest—to keep the Ripper mystery unsolved. For generations students of history and criminology have mulled over suspects, witness testimony, and crime scene circumstances. Unraveling the Whitechapel murders would engender an anticlimax. The Ripperologist newsletter and Cloak & Dagger Club might fold. Scores of amateur detectives would have to seek a new hobby. The wise consider journeys as meaningful as reaching destinations. Our fascination with the Ripper conundrum brings to mind a statement made by Amazing Stories magazine editor Ray Palmer at a 1977 UFO conference. "If we knew exactly what flying saucers were, ... we'd return to boredom and stop thinking ..."[15]

Endnotes

1 "Jack" might have made some of those puncture holes in the shawl with his knife. Others were cut out by scientists from Kings College, Cambridge in 2017. While filming the History Channel TV series "American Ripper," lawyer-author-broadcasting personality Jeffrey Mudgett evidently obtained permission from Russell Edwards to conduct tests on it. He wanted to determine whether or not his great-great-grandfather, serial killer Herman Webster Mudgett (aka H. H. Holmes), committed the Whitechapel murders. Jeffrey went to the length of exhuming g-g-grandpa from his concrete-fortified grave in Yeadon, Pennsylvania's Holy Cross Cemetery. University of Pennsylvania anthropologists collected DNA from the corpse's inner ear, and sent it to Kings College for analysis. Jeffrey also had a theory that wily "Holmes" had somehow escaped execution in 1896. So he and his siblings donated their DNA to confirm whether or not the male interred 121 years ago really was their ancestor. After all that hubbub and expense, Herman Mudgett turned out to be himself. He did not cheat the hangman. Nor did his DNA match that of Kate Eddowes' killer.

2 Wikipedia, Aaron Kosminski, op. cit. Jari Louhelainen Ph.D and David Miller Ph.D, "Forensic Investigation of a Shawl Linked to the Jack the Ripper Murders." Skeptics continue to doubt the veracity of Louhelainen's findings. Ripper expert Donald Rumbelow declared the shawl to be "of dubious origin," and added that the police report's inventory of Catherine Eddowes' possessions made no mention of it.

3 Kay Burgess, "DNA Row Over Ripper Identity 'Proof'," The Australian, September 9, 2014.

4 John E. Douglas and Mark Oldshaker, The Cases' That Haunt Us, Scribner, New York, 2000, pp. 79-80.

5 Wikipedia, Goulston St. Graffito. Various witnesses recorded different versions of the message. Researcher Martin Fido thought it the work of a semi-literate Cockney because of the double negatives and misspelling of "Jews" as "Juwes."

6 Ibid., Commissioner Charles Warren to Home Undersecretary Godfrey Lushington, November 6, 1888.

7 Ido Etrati, Haaretz (newspaper,) Tel Aviv, Israel, "Scientists Discover Gene That Predisposes Ashkenazi Jews to Schizophrenia," November 28, 2013. Schizophrenia affects approximately 1% of humanity. Dr. Ariel Darvasi of Jerusalem's Hebrew University and Dr. Todd Lencz of New York's Feinstein Institute for Medical Research collaborated on a study which found that Ashkenazi Jews, due to the prevalence of the NDST3 gene, have a 40% higher chance of suffering from schizophrenia than the general population.

8 Wikipedia, Aaron Kosminski, from Robert Anderson's The Lighter Side of My Official Life, as quoted by Paul Begg in Jack the Ripper: The Definitive History, Pearson Education, London, 2003, p. 269.

9 Ibid., This quotation comes from Sir Melville Macnaghten's notes, op. cit. Stewart P. Evans & Keith Skinner, The Ultimate Jack the Ripper Sourcebook: An Illustrated Encyclopedia, Constable & Robinson, London, 2000, p. 584.

10 www.casebook.com, Dr. Frederick Gordon Brown's autopsy report on the murder of Catherine Eddowes.

11 Robert Anderson, The Lighter Side of My Official Life, Hodder & Stoughton, London, 1910. Some Ripperologists have proposed Jewish cigar maker Hyam Hyams (1855-1913) as a Ripper suspect. Being 5'7", 33 years old at the time, depraved. mustachioed, dark-haired, and foreign-looking, he fit "Jack's" description. Hyams lived and worked in Whitechapel, within walking distance of all murder scenes. He happened to be the nephew of Eddowes' case witness Joseph Hyam Levy, who thought he spotted unstable Hyam talking to an English prostitute while dressed as a sailor. In any event Levy became uncooperative with police. According to the October 19, 1888 edition of The Evening News: "Mr. Joseph Levy is absolutely obstinate and refuses to give the slightest information, and he leaves one to infer that he knows something, but ... is afraid to be called on the inquest." Hyam Hyams was an alcoholic, epileptic, and schizophrenic with a history of domestic battery. He beat his wife repeatedly and once struck his mother in the head with a hatchet, seriously injuring her. On January 4, 1890, a court remanded him to Colney Hatch Asylum, where he remained until his death on March 22, 1913. Hyams' file characterized him as: "... noisy, threatening, and destructive ... He continually attacked other patients and members of staff, at one time creeping up behind a medical officer as he was passing through the ward, and stabbing him in the neck with a makeshift knife." I don't think Hyams was Jack the Ripper since his DNA did not match the Kosminski-Kaminski profile on Catherine Eddowes' shawl. Also, police did not arrest him for violent behavior until December 29, 1888, three weeks after Nathan Kaminski's apprehension. They obviously did not consider Hyams a Ripper suspect because he was intermittently released from custody--first on January 11, 1889, then again on September 19, 1889 after a second confinement for aberrant activity in August of that year. (See Mark King's article on him at casebook.org, Hyam Hyams.)

12 casebook.org. (Martin Fido, re: Nathan Kaminsky – "David Cohen.") Joseph Lawende probably shared Commissioner Charles Warren's belief that the arrest of a Jew for the Ripper murders would provoke violent anti-Semitic riots in London.

13 Wikipedia, Aaron Kosminski, Inspector Donald S. Swanson's marginal notes on page 138 of his copy of Sir Robert Anderson's copy of The Lighter Side of My Official Life.

14 Stewart Evans and Keith Skinner, The Ultimate Jack the Ripper Companion, Carroll & Graf, New York, 2000, p. 628, op. cit. London Globe, March 7, 1910.

15 David J. Halperin, Intimate Alien, The Hidden Story of the UFO, Stanford University Press, Stanford, CA, 2020, pp. 201-02.

CHAPTER 8:

Tottering Tumblety

Francis Tumblety still misbehaved in his sixties and seventies. Sometime in mid-November 1890 he took a train to Washington, D. C. and checked into the Myers Hotel. On the night of November 17th Detective Ned Horne arrested him for perverse conduct as he lurked in the shadows at 9th & Pennsylvania Avenue. Since a fleeing teenaged boy attracted Horne's attention, we can guess Tumblety's intent. Though apprehended as a "suspicious character,"[1] he escaped conviction once again, because his victim did not want to press charges.

The Washington Post published this item on November 19, 1890:

> Dr. Francis Tumblety was given a hearing in police court
> yesterday. He produced testimony as to his good character
> in years past, but there was strong circumstantial evidence of
> his recent suspicious conduct to show that Detective Horne
> was fully justified in placing him under arrest. Judge Miller
> was compelled to dismiss the case, but did so with reluctance
> ... The police will keep Tumblety under surveillance during
> his stay in Washington.[2]

This would be the third time since jumping bail in London that Tumblety had gotten into trouble for propositioning an adolescent male. Despite his record as a sexual predator, he had the gall to publish an article entitled "A Parent's Duty to the Young" in the June 9, 1892 edition of The Burlington Free Press.

Due to the ravages of syphilis and rheumatism, 61 year old Tumblety had slowed down considerably by 1891. Still a disciple of hydro-therapist Dr. Richard Barter, he vacationed in Hot Springs, Arkansas, Saratoga Springs, New York, and Bar Harbor, Maine. While in New York City, he patronized the bathhouses of Dr. E. P. Miller on Twenty-sixth St. and Dr. C. T. Ryan's Lafayette Baths on Lafayette Place.

Toward the end of his life Tumblety bounced around to and from Baltimore, Rochester, Hot Springs, New Orleans, and St. Louis. While in Rochester he usually stayed with niece Mary Fitzsimmons, daughter of his sister Alice who had died in 1883.

The Grim Reaper did not spare the Tumulty family between 1895 and 1898. Francis's sister Margaret Kelly died in Waterloo, New York on January 24, 1895; sister Elizabeth Powderly, also of Waterloo, passed away three months later on April 25, 1895; sister Mary Kavanagh suddenly dropped dead while visiting Dublin in January 1896.

Francis's trips to Rochester terminated following elder brother Lawrence's death on February 14, 1898. Larry had been his protector as a boy, counselor during young adulthood, and lifelong confidante—perhaps his only true friend.

Francis helped Lawrence purchase the house on Sophia St. (later renamed Plymouth Ave.) in Rochester which their mother Margaret had previously rented. Larry never married. He worked as a landscape gardener and nurseryman for over forty years. From the late 1860s until his death he earned extra income by taking in roomers. Around 1884 Larry traveled by rail to California to visit sister Jane Hayes in Vallejo, California.

Lawrence began suffering from dementia by age 77. He died in the winter of 1898 as a result of a fall which injured his head, neck, and back. To the chagrin of his nephews and nieces, Larry left most of his estate to Catholic charities. Nephews Michael Fitzsimmons, James Kavanagh, William Mahoney, and James P. Tumilty learned a lesson from that disappointing outcome, which prepared them for the demise of wealthier "Uncle Frank."

The earlier chapters of this book documented how Francis groomed himself immaculately in his younger years. That foppishness ended by the early 1890's when physical infirmities and depression began to overwhelm him.

In 1879 New York City court reporter Clement R. Bennett described Tumblety's Navy Commodore costume:

He wore a double-breasted, buttoned-up pea jacket, light (nankeen) pantaloons, a flashy necktie, cloth gaiters on his English box-toe shoes, a military … cap, with a gold cord lying upon the straight peak, and some loud jewelry …[3]

58 year old Francis Tumblety dressed in his naval officer's costume.
(Atchison, Kansas Daily Globe, December 15, 1888)

On June 12, 1900, the U. S. census enumerated Tumblety living in a widow's duplex: Francis Tumblety, 218-220 N. Liberty St, Baltimore, MD, (no age given), boarder, physician, bachelor, born in Maryland (sic), parents born in Ireland, zero months unemployed. Catherine Howard, owner, widow, 34, born Chicago, IL, no children, and her mother, Mary Coyle 54, widow, born in Ireland.

In early September 1900 nomadic Tumblety erred by wandering into Galveston, Texas right before the devastating hurricane of September 9, 1900 which unleased 145 miles per hour winds that claimed the lives of an estimated 9,000 people—almost a quarter of the city's population. According to The St. Louis Post-Dispatch, a flood swept Tumblety away, nearly drowning him.

> He floated about on a chicken coop until rescued by a tug boat, but his health was permanently impaired.[4]

After that traumatic experience Tumblety's heart, kidney, and arthritic complaints grew worse. Progressive invalidism prevented him from performing manual chores. Because it hurt to raise his arms and turn his head, simple tasks like getting dressed, shaving, and combing his hair became cumbersome. No longer a dandy, he dispensed with the services of valets. Responsibilities such as buying new clothes or having his laundry washed and pressed were neglected. Former fashion plate Francis gradually morphed into an unkempt old geezer with poor short-term memory and proneness to dizzy spells. When venturing out in public, he'd throw on any old garb, and clumsily smear pancake makeup over the syphilitic lesions on his face. By fall of 1900 Tumblety limped through Baltimore's streets after dark, looking like a frayed version of Quasimodo, hunchback of Notre Dame.

After a trip to Saratoga Springs, New York during the summer of 1902, Francis returned to Baltimore for a few weeks, then set off for St. Louis in November, where he'd stay for the remaining six months of his life. On April 26, 1903, Tumblety fell gravely ill and admitted himself to St. John's Hospital, 22nd & Morgan streets, run by the Sisters of Mercy. Because of his slovenly appearance, Mother Superior Mary Theresa ordered him to buy a new suit. Tumblety did so, but never wore it. He paid for a private room out of his own pocket, and assured her: "The only thing poor about me is my health."[5]

Tumblety's condition deteriorated. After dinner on May 24th an orderly helped him get dressed. He announced that he was going for a walk that evening, and did not want anyone to accompany him. Nursing nuns tried to dissuade him, but he insisted, and hobbled out of the hospital and down the street. Tumblety biographer Timothy Riordan surmised that this reckless foray might have been one last prowl in search of a sexual encounter. Another theory has it that, depressed by his disability, Francis intentionally tried to overexert himself in order to hasten his death. Upon returning to the hospital, he collapsed while mounting the building's granite front steps and fell forward. Orderlies picked Tumblety up, and carried him back to his bed. He'd suffered a broken nose and facial bruises. Hospital staff summoned Dr. A. V. L. Brokaw to reset Francis' nose and treat the contusions on his face. Tumblety died four days later on May 28, 1903. Dr. Francis A. Temm attributed his demise to heart failure, with Bright's Disease noted as contributory. Tumblety's death certificate incorrectly stated his marital status as "widower" and age as 82 (rather than 73).

St. Louis undertakers Cullinane Brothers embalmed Tumblety's corpse and shipped it to O'Reilly & Sons funeral parlor in Rochester. Following a requiem mass at St. Joseph's Roman Catholic Church, relatives planted him in the family plot at Holy Sepulchre Cemetery. Tumblety's last 812 mile rail trip from St. Louis to Rochester fit his roving lifestyle. We find him still traveling as a corpse on that final excursion to his grave.

Tumblety's Three Contested Wills

"Fortune Won by Herbs (the) Root of (a) Bitter Fight..."

Newspaper article title in The St. Louis Post Dispatch, June 28, 1903

DR. FRANCIS TUMBLETY.

This cartoonish drawing of Tumblety wearing what looks like a circus band
conductor's uniform appeared along with The St. Louis Post Dispatch article of June
28, 1903, which broke the news that New York relations had challenged his will.

Francis registered at St. John's Hospital under the alias "Frank
Townsend," but used his real name on May 16, 1903 when making the "St.
Louis will" with attorney Thomas D. Cannon of St. Louis's Campbell &
Thompson law firm, (who had been referred to him by hospital chaplain
Father John J. Conway). According to the June 26, 1903 edition of The
New York Times, Tumblety bequeathed $65,000. to the following eight
individuals:

$10,000. Jane Hayes (sister and only surviving sibling)

10,000. Mrs. Thomas Brady, Liverpool, (niece)

10,000. Mary Fitzsimmons (niece)

10,000. Cardinal James Gibbons, Archbishop of Baltimore

10,000. Archbishop John Ireland, St. Paul, Minnesota (Father John Conway, who'd formerly served in St. Paul, suggested that bequest)

5,000. Mrs. Annie Barrett Gibbs, Rochester, New York, (niece)

5,000. Jane Moore, Rochester, NY, (niece)

5,000. Mark A. Blackburn, New York City (former "coachman.")

St. Louis County Register of Wills Garrard P. Strode discovered that Tumblety's account with Henry Clews Banking House in New York held $138,000. (approximately $4.3 million in today's money).

Soon after Francis's burial, aggrieved relatives and their lawyers swooped into St. Louis like so many vultures. On behalf of passed-over upstate New York relatives, nephews Michael Fitzsimmons, James P Tumilty (a former New York Assemblyman), William L. Mahoney, James Kavanagh, et al., filed suit on January 16, 1904 claiming that their eccentric uncle was not of "sound mind and disposing memory, (nor) capable in law of making a valid will."[6] Judge McDonald ruled Francis Tumblety intestate for the undistributed balance of his estate, and ordered his will to be probated.

That process would only be the first round of a five year ordeal which dragged through Missouri courts until April, 1908. The City of St. Louis first had to fight off the Tumultys' request for a change of venue to New York. That issue was ultimately settled. New York State imposed a $7,000 transfer tax ($200,000 in today's money) for allowing Henry Clews & Co. to remit a check for $131,000 to the City of St. Louis's Trust Department.

It turned out that Francis had made two other wills. His Baltimore acquaintance, Major Joseph Ritner Kemp, came forward with the Maryland will which named different heirs. It was dated October 3, 1901, witnessed by lawyers Robert H. Simpson, Charles A. Simpson, and William Duval, but signed only with an "X." Interestingly, this document left $1,000. to The Home for Fallen Women of Baltimore City. Author Michael Hawley interpreted that gesture as an indication that Tumblety, soon to meet his Maker, wanted to atone for past wrongs against "ladies of the night."

While sporting flashy jewelry during a May, 1902 visit to New Orleans, Tumblety practiced false economy by checking into a rundown boarding house, with the result that a pipe-wielding ruffian assaulted and robbed him. Fearing he would not recover from his wounds, Francis entreated 25 year old Joseph Mitchell, whom he recently met at the city's Grand Opera House, to summon a Catholic priest. About twenty minutes later Mitchell returned with Father Gaffney. In their presence Tumblety willed $20,000. to California sister Jane Hayes, $20,000. to a nephew in Rochester, $20,000. to a New Jersey cousin, $20,000. to a New York man (probably Mark Blackburn), and another $20,000. to Joseph Mitchell. He directed Father Gaffney to donate the balance to Church-sponsored charities.

A St. Louis court threw out the Baltimore and New Orleans documents because they antedated the May 16, 1903 St. Louis will. Of course, Judge McDonald knew that a change of venue would have denied the city and State of Missouri estate tax revenue and court costs.

We can glean two distinct themes from Tumblety's St. Louis and New Orleans wills. He preferred female relatives to males; and wished to bequeath a substantial portion of his estate to Catholic philanthropies. Notice that he consulted priests—Father Gaffney in New Orleans and Father Conway in St. Louis—before dictating those wills. That inclination seems to support the notion that Tumblety wanted to leave a sizable portion of his assets to the Catholic Church. In June 1903 The St. Louis Post Dispatch reported:

> Lawyer (Thomas D.) Cannon who drew up the (St. Louis) will says Dr. Tumblety undoubtedly intended to give the remainder of his estate to charity, but ... the suddenness of his death prevented him from doing so.[7]

The Estate of Francis Tumblety Probate Proceedings

In 2017 documentary filmmaker Michael Sandknop ordered Francis Tumblety's bulky estate file from City of St. Louis Archives, which contained sworn testimony from 47 witnesses. Since most of those people, deposed under oath, had nothing to gain from their statements, we should be inclined to accept their declarations at face value. But the truth about Tumblety lies somewhere between the extremes of his own braggadocio and slurs of detractors.

The defense witnesses were banker Henry Clews who judged Francis still "a shrewd businessman (whose) mind (had been) unaffected"[8] by his final illness. Dr. Francis Temm, Dr. J. H. Ziegler, and other hospital employees believed he "showed deep religious feeling ... on his deathbed,"[9] which disposed him to charity.

Since Francis's nephews and nieces challenged his will, their witnesses' narratives portray him as a half-mad derelict, unable to think clearly.

The contestants' attorneys did not call anyone to the stand who had anything good to say about image-conscious Tumblety.

In 1901 Tumblety still affected nautical attire, but looked more like a pirate past his prime than Navy admiral. Daniel O'Donovan, proprietor of U. S. Engraving Co. in Baltimore testified:

> He gave me the impression from his clothes, which ... were
> very dirty and greasy, of being a sailor in hard luck.[10]

(Readers will recall that Tumblety sued O'Donovan in 1898 because of the shoddy printing job he'd done on the autobiography's last edition.)

With regard to Francis's hygiene and complexion, his New Orleans attorney J. M. Goodin did not mince words.

> His appearance was very dirty; his clothes were slovenly; from
> his face I judged that he had syphilis.[11]

Tumblety's barber in Hot Springs, Arkansas, B. McDavid stated:

> His hair and mustache were perfectly white, but he kept them
> blackened with a preparation ... of lard and charcoal that
> made him look very fierce.[12]

When Judge Gabriel Fernandez Jr. asked witness Richard S. Norris if Tumblety was clean, he replied: "No sir, he looked dirty, very filthy."[13]

Hot Springs tobacco shop owner Adolf Marx added:

> He was complaining often. He always pointed to his heart ...
> and would say he had heart trouble ... His clothes were not
> clean; his coat was shiny and soiled ... Anybody could see

that he had dye on his beard ..., sometimes hanging in little rows of his hair.[14]

Attorney Frank M. Widner Jr. remembered first meeting Tumblety in October, 1901. Having forgotten the name and room number of lawyer Robert H. Simpson, he stumbled into Widner's office, and asked where he could find the young man with light brown hair. (At that time Baltimore's five story Law Building contained dozens of offices.)

Robert H. Simpson and Richard S. Norris delivered the most shocking testimony. Simpson related this incident:

> He had a fainting spell in my office... I opened his coat and noticed he wore no suspenders; he was breathing very heavily; my brother was present. I opened his trousers ... and he seemed to be shaped like a woman; we picked him up and ... his trousers came down and I noticed he had a penis that was scarcely as large as the end of your finger ... (Later) I asked him the question whether or not he was a hermaphrodite; ... he asked, 'what do you ask that for?' I said your trousers came down and we saw everything you had. He said, 'do not ever tell that to anybody; that is a misfortune which has followed me all through my life; that is true.' Another characteristic about him was he had a voice like a girl ...[15]

At his deposition Richard S. Norris declared that in a boardinghouse during one Mardi Gras season Tumblety

> ... unbuttoned his pants, and showed me something, and told me he was not good. He was trembling and ... very nervous. He asked me to go to bed with him, that he enjoyed it just as

much as a woman ... Of course, I did not know at the time the difference between a morphadite ... So he got into bed and cocked his legs up, but I did not get down and look at him; I stood off ...; he insisted upon my having connection with him. I told him I would do this tomorrow; and he did everything, coaxed me, ... offered me money, and made me promise that I would be back the next morning at 10 o'clock ... (The next day) he threw me on the bed and we had quite a tussle. He (pulled) me on top of him, but I was a pretty handy youngster myself then, was a wild fellow and took all sorts of chances. I was on the money side, saw he was stuck on me, and said, 'I have got a price if you want me to do anything like that.' I went over to my friend Doyle about it, and he said, 'Why don't you take a trick (and) see how it goes.[16]

Others confirmed Tumblety's androgyny. Detective James Pryor observed that he "had the smallest hand and foot I ever saw on a man."15[17]

Mortician Fred Nash informed the court that Tumblety only had one testicle. That condition, known as monorchism, has been linked to creativity, emotional imbalance, hypersensitivity, intolerance of criticism, depression, and borderline personality.

After bashing Tumblety to the nth degree, the "prosecution" rested. On April 14, 1908 the court approved final distribution. After taxes, court costs, and lawyers' fees, twenty-five of Tumulty family members received a total of $47,000 on a share basis, determined by degree of consanguinity. For example, nephews and nieces received more than grand-nephews and grand-nieces. In essence, probating his will diverted the net estate balance from Roman Catholic charities to lawyers, relatives Tumblety didn't especially like, New York State, the City of St. Louis, and State of Missouri.

Two of the contestants did not live to spend their awards. Tumblety's nephew Michael Fitzsimmons died in April, 1907. Forty-eight year old William Mahoney passed away a few weeks after the April, 1908 settlement. His share of $2,400. ($71,000 in 2021 dollars) reverted to wife Lottie. Both of them had become impatient with the long delay in resolving this matter, and hired a Syracuse lawyer (who accomplished nothing.) Mrs. Mahoney then refused to pay her share for the services of Rochester attorneys Edwin C. Metcalf, George B. Draper, and John S. Leahy, who actually won the case. They retained Harlan W. Rippey, Esq. to sue Mrs. Mahoney. He won a judgment against her, thus collecting $347. in unpaid legal fees, which would today amount to $10,250.

Thus, ended the convoluted affairs of "Dr." Francis Tumblety.

Endnotes

1 Trenton Times, November 19, 1890.

2 Washington Post, November 19, 1890.

3 San Francisco Chronicle, November 20, 1888.

4 St. Louis Post Dispatch, June 28, 1903.

5 Ibid.

6 John S. Leahy, Esq.'s plea on behalf of the New York Tumultys --- James P. Tumilty, Michael Fitzsimmons, William L. Mahoney, James Kavanagh, et al., City of St. Louis Archives, January 16, 1904.

7 St Louis Post Dispatch, June 28, 1903.

8 Ibid.

9 Ibid.

10 Estate of Francis Tumblety Probate Proceedings, City of St. Louis Archives, Testimony of Daniel O'Donovan, March 16, 1905.

11 Ibid., Statement of J. M. Goodin, Esq.

12 Ibid., Statement of B. McDavid.

13 Ibid., Statement of Richard S. Norris, May 12, 1905.

14 Ibid., Statement of Adolf Marx.

15 Ibid., Statement of Robert H. Simpson, Esq, March 16, 1905.

16 Ibid., Statement of Richard S. Norris, May 12, 1905. Michael Hawley cited a 1998 study conducted by psychiatrists at Rotterdam's Erasmus University which found that 39% of hermaphrodites suffer from severe psychopathological disorders—nearly double the general population's rate. Cf. Hawley, p. 246.

17 Pittsburgh Chronicle & Telegraph, November 27, 1888.

CHAPTER 9:
Sinner Reforming at a Snail's Pace

"Every valley shall be exalted, and every mountain and hill made low; and the crooked shall be made straight, and the rough places plain."

Isaiah 40:4

After Auburn Prison released "Big Jim" Brady in August, 1888, he and Sophie got together. They traveled to Europe, worked as a crime team, and unlawfully married on December 11th (since Sophie's divorce from Ned Lyons had not yet gone into effect.) The only setback during this romantic adventure occurred when an alert French policeman spotted Sophie picking a man's pocket near the Arc d' Triomphe in Paris. Before a magistrate she produced letters of introduction which falsely identified her as Madame DeVarney, a rich American widow. The judge glanced at her bogus references, tossed them aside with the remark "I don't believe a word of this nonsense," and sentenced her to six weeks in dingy St. Lazare Prison.

In October 1890 forty-three year old Sophie's liaison with Jim Brady resulted in her seventh pregnancy. Sophia Madeline Brady was born in London on January 28, 1891. Soon thereafter Jim disappeared and presumably died. In the words of Sophie's biographer Shayne Davidson:

A compelling reason to believe that Brady did indeed die around 1891 is that after 1890 he wasn't involved in any crimes.[1]

Sophie claimed to have gone straight in 1889, but her sluggish rehabilitation process did not really commence until about 1912. By 1893 decreasing manual dexterity left her slower on the draw for pickpocketing and shoplifting. Therefore, she attempted to branch out. At that time the U. S. still had its Chinese Exclusion Act on the books. Sophie made a few thousand bucks by smuggling illegal Chinese aliens from Windsor, Canada to America. However, that venture into human trafficking ended on April 26, 1893 after police arrested her with an undocumented Chinese immigrant on a Detroit streetcar.

52 year old Sophie Lyons, in 1900, from the Smithsonian
Institution's National Portrait Gallery.

Sophie next opened a phony "marriage bureau" which advertised that it could match lonely men with "lovely young ladies (and) rich widows"[2] for a membership fee of $5. ($154. in today's currency). This enterprise generated steady income for a few months, but gradually disintegrated after dissatisfied customers complained to newspapers and police that it was a "bunko scheme," since no desirable females ever materialized. Sophie got off with little more than a cease and desist order, because most bureau members lived out of state, and none wanted to admit being lovelorn dupes in court. She dodged U. S. mail fraud charges by using a Canadian post office box for this scam.

Sophie garnered seed money for her Detroit real estate investments by going on a two-year European crime spree with lover Billy Burke between 1899 and 1901. This jaunt took them to London, Paris, Berlin, Vienna, Budapest, Prague, Rome, and other capitals. While in Rome the duo took time out for an audience with Pope Leo XIII, during which "he blessed Sophie and she kissed the hem of his robes."[3]

Sophie and Billy returned to Detroit in June, 1901 with seven trunks full of loot, consisting of jewelry, art works, "Parisian gowns," and other valuables. A month later she purchased two more rental properties with cash.

To take advantage of the crowds at Stockholm's 1912 Olympic Games, Billy and Sophie traveled there. On June 18th Stockholm police detained her for "casing" several jewelry stores. U. S. Consul General K. L. Harris arranged a deal to get the charges dropped in exchange for her deportation. That experience seemed to end Sophie's criminal career. Her real estate investments earned enough money. Then 64 years old, she finally recognized that it went against her own rational self-interest to risk imprisonment for unnecessary thefts..

In the past Sophie had made halting attempts to clean up her act. As early as April, 1884, right after her acquittal for the Ann Arbor Fair thefts, she gave speeches on the futility of crime at White's Grand Theater in Detroit. They were exercises by which she intended to talk herself into getting on the straight and narrow path. Those impromptu "sermons" eventually formed the basis of her 1913 book, Why Crime Does Not Pay.

In that work Sophie wrote—or narrated to a ghost writer—a diverting combination of fact and fable, including her own recollections, newspaper articles, secondhand accounts related by cronies, and just plain fibs. Although she tritely repeated the refrain "crime does not pay" at the end of every chapter, even inattentive readers could detect nostalgia for her exciting former life as a con artist and sneak thief. Sophie related the exploits of such colorful rascals as bank burglar Jimmy Hope, confidence man "Swell" Robinson, dishonest locksmith "Dutch Dan" Watson, Irish crime lord John Grady, and one of her own mentors, New York City's "Queen of Crime," Frederika Weisner Mandelbaum (1826-1894).

Frederika "Marm" Mandelbaum (1826-1894), New York City's "Queen of Crime." Sketch by Valerian Gribayedoff, 1887 from Recollections of a New York City Police Chief by George W. Walling, Caxton Book Concern, Ltd., New York, NY, 1887.

Sophie treated readers to an inside look at the operations of Marm, whom she viewed with ambivalent feelings of admiration and repulsion. A criminal genius, Frederika Mandelbaum never personally stole anything after the age of 22. She delegated that hazardous task to less intelligent subordinates.

In 1850 Frederika and her husband Wolfe emigrated to New York from Kassel, Germany, where they'd toiled as "junk peddlers." By 1862 the couple acquired enough capital to open a pawn shop on Rivington St. in Manhattan's Lower East Side. Marm always functioned as the brains of the outfit. She quickly purchased the building they rented on Rivington St., then the one next door, which was converted into a variety store and warehouse for stolen goods. Since bothersome customers irritated Marm, she ordered husband Wolfe and manager Herman Stoude to run the retail side. She barricaded herself in a rear office behind a reinforced steel cage. Because Mrs. Mandelbaum faced danger from both police and fellow crooks, she put elaborate security precautions in place. Besides employing armed guards and installing an alarm system, she had trap doors built, as well as a false chimney which concealed the dumbwaiter that facilitated her escape with gems and money to secret rooms with sliding walls and hidden safes.

Because so many of the pilfered rings, bracelets, and watches that came her way were engraved with initials or personal inscriptions (e.g. "to my beloved Fanny, love Oscar,") unsentimental Marm had them melted down into gold bars.

Mrs. Mandelbaum had a conference room next to her office, which she used to plan heists with professional thieves. According to Sophie,

It became a clearing house for ... larceny – big and small. (Criminals) hung about the premises as if it were an

employment agency, waiting for the 'boss' to find a job suited
to their particular talents.[4]

Frederika Mandelbaum favored inside jobs. She hired "tramps and
peddlers"[5] to act as scouts. Household servants were bribed to provide maps
of masters' houses, information about vacations, and hiding places where
valuables were stashed. Sometimes disloyal butlers, coachmen, and maids
conveniently left cellar doors and windows unlocked. For cash payments
dishonest store employees disclosed building plans, work schedules, the
locations of safes, and peak seasons when there would be more money and
inventory on the premises. When the cops applied too much heat, Marm
dispatched an emissary with a satchel full of cash to pay off Democrat pols
at Tammany Hall.

Both a workaholic and gourmand, Marm unwound by hosting lavish
parties in the banquet halls of Manhattan's best restaurants. In addition to
her underworld and Tammany Hall cronies, she would invite Broadway
stars and jaded Gotham socialites to these feasts. Seven course dinners with
the choicest delicacies and finest wines were served, while string quartets
played background music.

Frederika "Marm" Mandelbaum (far right) hosting a banquet at Delmonico's Restaurant in Manhattan. Drawing by Valerian Gribayedoff from George W. Walling's Recollections of a New York Chief of Police, 1887.

Mrs. Mandelbaum's downfall occurred in 1884 after her associate Mary "Molly" Holbrook (an old friend of Sophie's) was busted for shoplifting. Marm refused to pay her legal expenses because she hadn't authorized that caper. It had been one of Molly's personal jobs. Marm didn't like hangers-on playing her for a sucker. She knew Molly had pinched those items for her own use, and had no intention of splitting half with "the house." It would set a bad precedent to let her slide. Then every schmuck in the gang would try to pull that cheap trick. Therefore, she had to put her foot down. It was the principle of the thing. Marm later regretted her punctilious correctness in this matter.

Claustrophobic Molly Holbrook hated jail. No wonder they called Lower Manhattan's Halls of Justice The Tombs. It seemed like hell. She shook with fear, cried, got hysterical, then furious. Her face reddened and became contorted with rage. She screamed: "I'll fix that goddamned bitch!"

Molly soon made a deal with District Attorney Peter B. Olney to squeal on long-time boss Marm in exchange for leniency. Concerned about her unsuitability as a witness, he hired Pinkerton detectives to infiltrate Mandelbaum's fencing racket for the purpose of gathering more concrete evidence. A few weeks later Olney indicted Marm, her son Julius, and manager/paramour Herman Stoude. No trial took place. All three of the accused jumped bail and fled to Canada. The Mandelbaums absconded with an estimated one million dollars' worth of cash, jewelry, silver, and gold (i.e., 30 million in 2021 dollars).

Marm lived out her final ten years as a depressed exile in Hamilton, Ontario. When her daughter Anna died in November 1885, Mrs. Mandelbaum snuck back to New York in disguise. From a distant vantage point desolate Marm watched as Anna's coffin was lowered into her grave. Frederika Mandelbaum never again returned to the U. S. But after dying on February 27, 1894 her remains were buried next to husband Wolfe and daughter Anna in Queens County's Union Field Cemetery.

In Why Crime Does Not Pay Sophie shared interesting observations about her profession. Among thieves, pickpockets occupied the lowest rung on the ladder, with bank robbers on top. Adopting the "Robin Hood" image, and "easy-come-easy go" philosophy, cavalier outlaws tended to be more generous than their law-abiding counterparts. Bipolar male criminals generally blew their "earnings" on hedonistic pursuits such as gambling, whoring, and boozing, while many female lawbreakers held onto their ill-gotten gains.

Wanton Sophie Van Elkan Harris Lyons Brady Burke herself was obviously attracted to bad boys. She argued that women as a whole found desperadoes sexy. "Criminals successful and unsuccessful rarely lack women to love them."[6]

Sophie claimed she colluded with confidence woman Marion E. Gratz La Touche (alias "Carrie Morse") in the fraudulent Ladies' Investment Bureau plot which pledged 25% interest to female depositors. She had no problem swindling rich women. However, when an elderly widow brought in her life savings of $500, "virtuous" Sophie advised her to put it right back into her legitimate bank. Author Shayne Davidson exposed that story as a lie, since La Touche's swindle occurred in 1882 while Sophie chilled behind bars in Detroit. (Marion LaTouche received a relatively light sentence after her June, 1884 trial, and continued operating as a confidence woman until 1917.)

Sophie's account of a Mount Sterling, Kentucky bank robbery twisted truth beyond recognition. On May 27, 1892, the circus came to town. Sophie and Billy Burke showed up to take advantage of the distraction conjured by its parade of acrobats, clowns, and exotic animals. When all of Traders Deposit Bank's employees congregated outside the building to watch this spectacle, Sophie signaled Billy by waving her handkerchief. He dashed into the bank, pulled $4,600. out of the cashier's drawer, and ran out the front door. A teller saw Burke's antics through the building's plate glass window, and prevented his escape. Other employees summoned Mount Sterling's sheriff. A judge later sentenced Billy to five years in prison. Sophie got only six months for aiding and abetting. In Why Crime Does Not Pay she embellished this simple tale of a bank job gone wrong into a full-blown soap opera. Sophie changed Billy's name to "Tom Bigelow" and declared that Kentuckians would have lynched poor "Tom" if she hadn't made a scene by hugging him and begging for his life to be spared. While back in jail Sophie and "Tom" witnessed a brute named Murphy Logan stab his cellmate Charlie Steele to death. The mob reassembled, dragged Logan out to the village hanging tree, lynched him, then riddled his corpse with bullets. That overheated melodrama never occurred.

Crook with a Heart and her Troubled Offspring

Despite her rough exterior, aging Sophie sympathized with down-and-outers. Ignoring protests from prejudiced neighbors, she rented one of her properties to African-American philanthropist Mary E. McCoy who opened the McCoy Home for Colored Children in 1908. When a Detroit landlord evicted the destitute Wheeler family from their apartment, Sophie allowed them to live rent-free in her property at 51 23rd St. She championed prison reform, campaigned against capital punishment, and provided financial aid to both jail inmates and ex-cons. In 1916 Sophie promised to donate land at 24th & Lafayette St. in Detroit to the Pathfinders Club of America for a proposed building dedicated to teaching moral principles to the children of prisoners. The club appreciated her generosity, but declined the offer—not wanting to manage such a facility.

In December, 1919 Sophie gave Detroit House of Correction $100. ($1,579. adjusted for inflation) so prisoners could enjoy a special Christmas dinner. She sent checks for $500. ($7,900. in 2021 currency) to both Sing Sing and Auburn prisons so internees would receive Christmas gifts.

After the publication of Why Crime Does Not Pay, Sophie went on a 6-month world tour in 1913 which took her to England, France, Germany, Turkey, Palestine, Russia, Persia, and other countries. Eleven years later she refuted her book's title by dying wealthy with an estate valued at $241,766. (3.8 million in today's money).

George Lyons was not the only child who suffered ill effects from his parents' criminality. Florence and Victor both changed their "Lyons" surname to avoid being associated with Ned and Sophie.

Eight year old Victor remembered crying when the jury foreman in his mother's 1881 Michigan State Fair theft case announced the guilty verdict. He experienced bullying for being the son of thieves at both

Assumption College in Canada and Detroit's Home for the Friendless orphanage. During his teenaged years police officer William Somerville and his wife Elizabeth kindly took him into their household.

In July 1895 Victor, who had legally changed his name to Carleton C. Mason, traveled to Philadelphia's League Island Naval Base and enlisted in the Navy for three years. The Navy trained him as an electrician's mate, and assigned him to the U. S.S. New Orleans, which saw action off Cuba's coast near Santiago during the Spanish-American War. He was later transferred to Admiral George Dewey's flagship, the U. S.S. Olympia. In 1898 Carleton shipped over for another three years.

Petty officer first class Carleton C. Mason received an honorable discharge in 1901, then moved to the Boston area, where he first worked as an electrician, then as a pool hall manager. On November 6, 1903, members of the Charlestown, Massachusetts Masonic Lodge initiated him into Freemasonry.

In 1910 Carleton, who remained a lifelong bachelor, decided to move to Washington State. On his way out west he visited Sophie and sister Florence in Detroit. After reaching Seattle, he initially lived in a rooming house at 601 Seventh Ave., and secured employment as an electrician. Within a few years Carleton resided in an apartment at 1625 Boylston St., worked as a customs broker, and joined the Elks Club.

Carleton's health began to deteriorate in 1920 due to kidney trouble and arteriosclerosis. His condition possibly stemmed from exposure to asbestos, combined with smoking and drinking. (Prohibition endangered the lives of drinkers by ushering in the heyday of bathtub gin and wood alcohol whiskey.) Carleton died in Spokane on March 5, 1922, one month shy of his 48th birthday.

After attending his funeral in Spokane, Sophie shipped her son's body back to Detroit for burial. Friends observed that she would tearfully speak aloud to "Victor" during visits to his grave in Woodmere Cemetery.

In Why Crime Does Not Pay, Sophie—like Tumblety and other writers of that era—appended numerous complimentary letters from leading citizens such as journalist Herbert Kaufman, Reverend Ferdinand Grentzkampf, and Grand Army of the Republic Post Commander James H. Everett. The final two pages her book featured a letter from Carleton (signed "Victor") in which he expressed sympathy for Sophie's anti-capital punishment stance, and praised her for teaching him good values.

> While our lives have been lived apart, I still have the most
> beautiful recollection of my Angel Mother teaching me to
> lisp my baby prayers. You have the assurance of your son that
> he has never forgotten those words of wisdom, and I regret
> others have not done so, because a mother can impress the
> minds of her babies with the principles which (will bring)
> our people and the whole world ... to a higher plane of
> civilization.[7]

Carleton's sisters would have winced—if not gagged—at the appellation "Angel Mother."

Eldest daughter Florence, the only child who stayed in Detroit, took the brunt of Sophie's abuse. In 1883 the 15 year old girl aged out of London, Ontario's Catholic orphanage and returned home. Sophie had begun to support herself as a teenager, and felt her sensitive daughter could do likewise. She arranged for Florence to live in an apartment at 4th & Michigan Ave. Finding the unit filthy when they arrived, Sophie ordered her to clean it up while she went out on an errand. Florence knocked on the landlady's apartment door and asked to borrow cleaning supplies. The grouchy old crone refused. When Sophie came back and saw that the dirty flat had not been swept, she exploded, cursing and striking Florence, then throwing her out onto the street.

The weeping 15 year old girl trudged through Grand Circus Park, not knowing what she would do. Providentially, Florence bumped into Bertha Robinson, one of her classmates from St. Mary's Academy. Bertha brought her home. Her widowed mother, Rebecca Pearce Robinson, allowed Florence to stay there indefinitely in exchange for doing housekeeping chores.

Within two weeks Sophie discovered her daughter's whereabouts, and stormed over to the Robinsons' house at 109 Adams Avenue. Instead of thanking Rebecca Robinson for feeding and sheltering Florence, she verbally abused her and threatened legal action. After that ugly scene, the hapless teenager became homeless again.

Either Mrs. Robinson or someone else informed Father Ernest Van Dyke of nearby St. Aloysius parish of Florence's plight. He obtained work for her as a live-in chambermaid at Detroit diocese's House of Good Shepherd Home for Girls.

To conceal her parentage from prospective employers, Florence used the last name "Edwards" instead of "Lyons." Between 1885 and 1903 she worked as a nanny. Most people perceived Florence as polite and religious. Those aware of her background wondered how such a refined young lady could be the daughter of two criminals.

Nonetheless, Sophie constantly demeaned Florence as a "chump." Queen of the Burglars author Shayne Davidson explained:

Sophie disapproved of Florence working as a nanny or maid for wealthy families because she viewed this menial work as beneath her daughter's ... abilities ...[8]

In the summer of 1901 when ten year old Madeline Brady came to Detroit for a visit, Sophie asked Florence to look after her. That assignment, of course, led to conflict. Florence refused to obey Sophie's command to give the child cold baths every morning. Although anyone who could read a newspaper knew of Sophie's notoriety, she accused Florence of telling Madeline all about her scandalous career. So the "joyous" reunion only provoked more dissension between mother and daughter.

For decades Sophie and Florence alternated between periods of hostility and reconciliation. Things went from bad to worse in September 1903 when Florence married Joseph C. Bauer, a man fourteen years younger than herself, whom Sophie described as a "drunken teamster" with checkered employment history. Florence delivered daughter Esther Bauer—Sophie's only grandchild—on September 10, 1904.

Jealous and abusive Joseph Bauer often assaulted Florence, leaving her with facial bruises and black eyes In the course of one ferocious beating he broke her right arm. Florence filed for divorce in July, 1907, and changed her married surname to "Bower." On July 14, 1917, she remarried Bauer, but separated from him again in 1925 when he reverted to his old ways. The State of Michigan issued the couple's final divorce decree on April 18, 1929.

Sophie refused to help Florence during her marital woes, declaring that her daughter wed Bauer without her "knowledge and consent."[9] Streetwise Sophie had instantly sized up Joe as a bum, and was incredulous that her naïve daughter couldn't see through him. Letting Schadenfreude get the best of her, she thought Florence deserved to pay the price for her bad judgment. Only hard knocks would wise her up. Although Sophie's own decisions to marry four crooks and pursue a criminal career hadn't been especially enlightened, she seemed to revel in her half-Irish, convent-educated daughter's dumb life choices.

At the nadir of their relationship in November, 1908, Florence tried to raise pennies for herself and four year daughter Esther by grinding a hand organ in front of Detroit's main public library. One day Sophie, "dressed in silks and diamonds passed by, ... turned to her companion, ... and said 'that woman is a fake.' "[10]

Sophie could not understand Florence's lack of chutzpah. To a Detroit News reporter she ranted: "I should have had my daughters taught to wash dishes, sew, and do housework, instead of sending them to the best schools ..."[11]

Sophie had given birth to Florence, Lottie, and Madeline, but didn't actually raise them. To her consternation they grew up to be clueless "shiksas" who never learned basic survival skills. This unsympathetic attitude toward her daughters apparently stemmed from the parental abuse she suffered as a child. Emotionally scarred Sophie couldn't bestow maternal love that she herself had never received.

From 1908 to 1912 Florence attempted to make up with her mother by writing conciliatory letters, but Sophie scrawled "return to sender" on most of them. In one of her epistles Florence prophetically wrote: "Do not cast me aside. Some day you will call me back."[12]

Sophie's Final Days and Beleaguered Estate

Sophie regularly ate lunch in the restaurant of her tenant Arshag Andonian at 3350 West Fort St. On March 25, 1924, three young hoodlums burst into the place, and ordered Mr. Andonian and Sophie into a back room. One of them shoved Sophie under a table and kicked her. Arshag Andonian entreated them not to assault his "mother." Sophie pretended to faint.

This dopey trio stole $50. cash and a watch from luncheonette proprietor Andonian, but ignored "Armenian old lady" Sophie, who wore rings worth thousands under her gloves, and had a thick roll of five, ten, and twenty dollar bills in her purse.

A few days later—after a shoot-out, which claimed the life of Detroit cop Benjamin Montie—police apprehended perpetrators Gene Murray and Charlie Howe of the Robbers' Roost gang. Sophie identified them on April 3rd.

That incident shook her up. Sophie admitted to newspaper reporters the folly of wearing diamonds in public at her age, and vowed to put them into her bank's safety deposit box.

Between 1912 and 1924 Sophie and daughter Florence alternately clashed and made peace. Because her spelling and punctuation skills weren't up to snuff, Sophie occasionally paid Florence to act as her social secretary, answering correspondence and assisting with property management. As she began to ail from high blood pressure and depression following the death of husband Billy Burke from a stroke on October 25, 1919, Sophie became more patient with Florence.

On April 30, 1924, over dinner at Hotel Tuller, mother and daughter ironed out their differences. Sophie assured Florence that she was one of her will's chief beneficiaries. They discussed plans for her to become more involved with the real estate holdings, and bring mentally ill Madeline home from England.

In the early 1920s Sophie lived in a two-family dwelling at 908 23rd St. On the morning of May 7, 1924 her upstairs tenant Gertrude Antle let in three young men who said they wanted to talk to "Mrs. Burke" about renting one of her properties. A few moments later Gertrude heard Sophie exclaim: "No! Don't! Leave me alone!"[13]

Those guys might have been gang members who were attempting to discourage Sophie from testifying against Gene Murray and Charlie Howe in their upcoming trial. In any event, Sophie passed out and collapsed onto the floor. Alarmed by her condition, they called police, and remained by her side until help arrived. Police officers summoned Dr. E. L. Campau. He found no "marks on her that would indicate violence,"[14] and believed she'd suffered a stroke due to chronic high blood pressure. An ambulance transported Sophie to Grace Annex Hospital where she died at 4:30 PM. Coroner James Burgess agreed with Dr. Campau's diagnosis. He waived an autopsy and ruled cerebral hemorrhage her cause of death.

Sophie first made her will in 1920, then revised it following the death of 47 year old son Victor in March 1922. She appointed Judge Ira Jayne executor of her estate and designated Detroit Trust Co. as co-trustee. The will dispersed her assets to individuals and charities as follows:

$45,000. daughter Florence

2,000. daughter Lottie

2,000. daughter Madeline

2,000. Detroit politician Sherman Littlefield

1,000. Detroit House of Correction (to buy a Steinway piano)

100. younger sister Mary Rohrs

100. granddaughter Esther Bower

50. (supposedly reformed) child murderer Jesse Pomeroy

Sophie set aside another $120,000. (1.9 million today) for The Sophia Lyons Memorial Fund, a philanthropy dedicated to the reformation of criminals and welfare of their families. She envisioned the construction and establishment of a model "house of refuge" to educate and care for imprisoned offenders' children.

Things did not go as planned. Daughter Lottie, who resided somewhere in England, could not be located. Beginning in 1897 she'd worked as a singer and actress, under the stage name "Lotta Belmont," however her show business career fizzled by 1901. For a while Lottie supported herself by teaching languages. But from 1921 until her death in April, 1935 at age 59, she drifted from one poorhouse to another.

In 1882 when Sophie "rescued" Lottie from adoption, she resisted, saying: "No, I do not like you, because you are a thief. You are not my mother at all!"[15] She would probably have been better off remaining with the family of would-be adoptive parents John and Mary Catherine Doyle. Florence Lyons Bower remembered Sophie saying in later years that Lottie always thought she was "too good" for her.

Because they could not notify Lottie about Sophie's bequest, administrators of the estate divided it, with court approval, between Florence and Madeline in 1929.

Madeline had also fallen on hard times. When Sophie ceased supporting her in 1908, the 17 year old girl managed to secure employment as private secretary to Lady Pembroke in Wiltshire. Sophie visited Madeline in Paris circa 1912, and paid for her passage to the U. S. in December, 1914. During that visit she claimed a $400. inheritance ($11,000. today) from the estate of Aunt Mary Ann Brady, older sister of her father, "Big Jim" Brady. Referring to Madeline as "Sophie Brady" (her baptismal name), The New York Tribune printed this account of her January 22, 1915 testimony in Newark, New Jersey's Orphans' Court.

Miss Sophie Brady, daughter of Sophie Lyons, a notorious woman criminal, ... took the stand ... Very Parisian and garbed in a long drab cape and chic black plush hat, the young woman told the story of her life. 'I spent my girlhood days in a convent in Paris, ... little dreaming what sort of woman my mother had been. Life was very happy there. I often inquired about my mother, but could find out little. Then many years ago, ... she came over. It was the first time I had seen her since I was a little girl and, of course, I scarcely remembered her. She asked me about myself and told me that I was to be educated in England and Germany. Then she went away. I left the convent and returned to London. I went to school there and later went to Germany, studying art and music. ... I spent a short time in your country. But I was glad to get back to Paris. I became a governess and then a stenographer. Then the war started and I was out of work.[16]

Madeline returned to France in February 1915. At some point she adopted older sister Lottie's stage surname "Belmont," and was believed to have volunteered for the war effort as a nurse or ambulance driver. Madeline suffered a nervous breakdown in May, 1918 and was admitted to London's Royal Bethlehem Hospital (aka "Bedlam") with a diagnosis of dementia praecox (schizophrenia). Without effecting any improvement in her condition, Bedlam discharged Madeline on October 15, 1919. She soon entered Newington Workhouse before being transferred to a series of insane asylums.

In March 1925 the staff of Horton Psychiatric Hospital learned that Madeline had family in Detroit. A solicitor for that institution contacted Florence Lyons Bower, who informed him of Sophie's death and Madeline's

$2,000. legacy. That phone conversation sparked a challenge to Sophie's will. In 1929 Horton Hospital prevailed, thus increasing Madeline's inheritance from $2,000. to $42,500. (approximately $682,000. today). According to public records Madeline never recovered her sanity, and died in Banstead Hospital near Epsom on August 27, 1963 at the age of 72.

During probate proceedings attorneys for Madeline's trust called several witnesses who characterized Sophie as mentally deranged. Among them were neighbor Minna Carpenter, prison matron Emma Betzing, plumber George Ellis, tenant Mrs. William Snell, contractor Duncan Graham, and psychiatrist Dr. Arnold Jacoby. Mrs. Snell remembered that one day she knocked on Sophie's door to pay her monthly rent. From within Sophie cried: "Go away! Go away! I can't see anybody today!"[17] Those spells of melancholy isolation could last as long as four days. Emma Betzing testified that while incarcerated at Detroit's House of Correction, Sophie raved maniacally in fits of fury, tried to starve herself, and attempted suicide. Parroting the textbook definition of mental incompetence, the plaintiffs' expert witness Dr. Arnold Jacoby pronounced her will,

> The product of a ... disordered, abnormal and unsound mind, having no conception of her duties ... to her own children, and possessed (of) deranged ... ideas respecting crimes and criminals.[18]

As of 1929, after paying legatees, estate taxes, and lawyers' fees, a balance of well over $100,000. (1.6 million in 2021 dollars) still sat in the estate's account with Detroit Trust Company. Though executor Ira Jayne and the bank did nothing to realize Sophie's charitable objectives, they continued to milk her estate until 1946, accruing more than $70,000. in fees (1.3 million adjusted for inflation). Declaring her house of refuge idea unfeasible after 22 years of "study," Jayne closed out the estate, claiming to have donated its depleted remnant to "established charities in the approved manner."[19]

Other forms of malaise accompanied the dissolution of Sophie's estate. Although she had at least seven kids, only daughter Florence produced a child. Esther Bauer Johnson (1904-1981) wed auto factory auditor William T. Johnson in 1925, but they never had any children. Thus, Sophie's genealogical line of descent died with Esther on January 18, 1981.

Sophia Lyons Burke's real estate empire followed a similar boom to bust pattern. In 1890 the Michigan lake port of Detroit boasted a population of 205,000. It flourished as a center for ship and carriage building. After the automobile's advent, "Motor Town" expanded rapidly. Its population increased to over 1.7 million by 1940. Independently-owned machine shops, auto glass works, and sheet metal foundries sprung up to fabricate components for the big car manufacturers.

Shortly after Ford Motor Company's founding in 1899, Detroit became increasingly polluted with smoke and noise. Auto industry executives, lawyers, and other upper middle class professionals headed for the suburbs of Grosse Pointe and Bloomfield Hills, transforming Detroit into a largely proletarian city.

"Motown's" nature as a single industry town—utterly dependent upon auto manufacturing—subjected it to the vagaries of that business. A monopolistic tendency caused minor players such as Packard, Studebaker, Pierce-Arrow, Hudson, Nash, etc. to either go under or be absorbed by the Big Three: Ford, General Motors, and Chrysler.

The restrictive Immigration Act of 1924 triggered a labor shortage in Detroit, which heavily relied on Polish, Irish, German, and Italian immigrants to man the assembly lines. Auto makers began recruiting

African-American employees from the rural south. Worker shortages during World War II gave further impetus to the Great Migration.

Meanwhile, the United Auto Workers union's rise motivated vehicle makers to move out of Detroit. The U.A.W. fomented numerous strikes in the 1930s, '40s, and '50s, which disrupted production. Higher wages and benefits for assembly-line personnel rendered American cars less competitively-priced on the world market. Tired of being harassed by the U.A.W., Ford, Chrysler, and GM fast-tracked efforts to exit "Motown" by the late 1950's. They constructed plants in Mexico, Canada, and anti-union southern states. The level of their disinvestment may be gauged by Ford's withdrawal from the city. In 1930 the company employed 90,000 Detroit citizens, but only 30,000 in 1960, and 6,000 by 1990.

Racial tensions spiked. In 1943 Franklin Delano Roosevelt's administration built the Sojourner Truth Project at Nevada and Fenelon streets. A white mob gathered to prevent African-Americans from moving in. Detroit police and National Guard tried to restore order, but violence escalated on June 20th in the Belle Isle section, resulting in 34 killed, 433 injured, and 2 million dollars' worth of property damage.

Skipping ahead twenty-four years, African-American rioting during the summer of 1967 claimed 43 lives (mostly Blacks), injured 467, and left 388 families homeless. 2,500 stores were vandalized, looted, or set on fire. Over 1,000 businesses closed down without reopening.

White flight began in earnest after that devastation. 67,000 whites moved out of Detroit in 1967, 80,000 in 1968, and 46,000 in 1969. The city's population dropped from a peak of 1.8 million in 1950 to 677,000 by 2010.

In 2012 sociologists counted 70,000 abandoned commercial buildings, 31,000 vacant dwellings, and 90,000 trash-strewn yards. Residents referred to multi-acre plots of windblown high grass where homes used to stand as "urban prairies." That year the average market value for a 3-bedroom Cape Cod house in Detroit sunk below $10,000. Mayor Dave Bing proposed that 25% of the city be demolished in order to "right-size" it. Servicing extensive stretches of sparsely inhabited areas had put a strain on the city's fire and police departments, as well as local electric, natural gas, and water companies.

In 2011 the FBI declared Detroit America's most dangerous metropolis, with a violent crime rate of 2,700 per 100,000 people (ten times higher than New York City.) Foreign nations issued travel alerts equating "Motown" with Somalia, Haiti, Sudan, and other failed states.

Approximately half of the city's homeowners defaulted on property taxes in 2012. On July 18, 2013, Emergency Manager Kenneth Orr filed the largest Chapter 9 municipal bankruptcy proceeding in U. S. history, citing debts of 18.5 billion dollars owed to more than 100,000 creditors.

Long story short, Sophie's estate sold off all of her properties before the bottom fell out of Detroit's real estate market. Nevertheless, it seemed symbolic of her distraught legacy that none of the forty-some houses she owned in the 23rd & Fort St. area survived. In the 1970s that neighborhood resembled bombed-out Dresden. Since then all structures have been razed, leaving a barren paved-over area, dotted with weed-choked lots and randomly dispersed heaps of rubble.

Sophie Lyons Burke turned to religion in her final years. During an interview with a newspaper reporter in 1913, she picked up a well-worn Jewish prayer book and read her favorite psalm of thanksgiving: "Thou, O Lord, hast always been gracious to me, and often sent me joys when I did least deserve them. For all this abundance I humbly thank Thee."[20]

THE TUMBLETY-LYONS CONNECTION

We know Sophie loaded her autobiography with tall tales, but some of its anecdotes strike us as plausible. While colluding with future husband Billy Burke in Paris circa 1900, she helped engineer the theft of a jewelry-filled suitcase belonging to Mrs. P. J. Lorillard, wife of the tobacco company heir. Sophie learned that Mrs. Lorillard rued the loss of a framed photograph of her deceased son much more than the purloined jewelry. Posing as a hotel detective, Sophie contacted Mrs. Lorillard and returned the picture. The bond that connected those two women from different worlds was grief over the death of a son.

Reflections on the Synchronicities

Dr. Carl Gustav Jung and others have defined "synchronicities" as meaningful coincidences which convey cryptic messages from the lower spiritual realm into our physical world. A remarkable number of these signs-from-beyond linked Tumblety and Lyons.

Many dissimilarities certainly existed between Sophie Lyons and Francis Tumblety. She was female, heterosexual, and Jewish; he male, homosexual, and Roman Catholic. Sophie favored real estate investments, whereas rolling stone Tumblety didn't want to bother with brick and mortar building repair bills, property taxes, insurance premiums, and annoying tenants.

Yet we find astonishing parallels in the lives of these adversaries. Both emigrated from abroad to the U.S., indulged in sexual promiscuity, were frequently arrested and jailed; traveled compulsively, attended papal audiences, donated to philanthropic causes, delivered public lectures, wrote self-glorifying autobiographies packed with fulsome testimonials, died rich, and had their wills contested. During probate hearings for their estates, multiple witnesses came forward to bash them, shattering their reputations like pinatas.

Both Francis and Sophie were crime victims in old age. Thieves forcibly entered Tumblety's Hot Springs, Arkansas hotel room on April 17, 1891 and stole $6,000. worth of jewelry and bonds ($145,000 today.) In May, 1902 a thug attacked, seriously injured, and robbed elderly Francis on a New Orleans street.

In July, 1916 conman Frederick Lehner, posing as a Hungarian count with Hollywood connections, rooked Sophie out of $600. ($15,300. 2021 dollars) by promising to make Why Crime Does Not Pay into a movie. Though Buffalo police arrested Lehner a few days later, he'd already spent most of the cash. During the summer of 1922 burglars broke into Sophie's home and carried off diamonds and bonds valued at $19,500. ($320,000. in 2021 dollars.). At the end of March, 1924, five weeks before her death, three bandits roughed her up in a Detroit luncheonette.

Both Francis and Sophie became depressed in their final years, and sought solace in religion. Ironically, the sworn foes had more in common than they thought.

Endnotes

1 Shayne Davidson, The Queen of the Burglars: The Scandalous Life of Sophie Lyons, Exposit, Jefferson, NC, 2020, p. 85.

2 Ibid., p. 117.

3 Ibid., p. 133, Cf. The Boston Post, June 6, 1901.

4 Sophie Lyons, Why Crime Does Not Pay, The Star Co., J. S. Ogilvie Publishing Co., New York, NY, 1913, p. 195.

5 Ibid., p. 193.

6 Ibid., p. 203.

7 Ibid., p. 277.

8 Davidson, p. 126.

9 Ibid., p. 142, op. cit. Detroit News, November 20, 1908.

10 Ibid.

11 Ibid., 142, op. cit. Detroit Free Press, November 20, 1908.

12 Ibid., p. 143, op. cit. Detroit News, November 20, 1908.

13 Ibid., p. 168, op. cit. Detroit Free Press, May 8, 1924.

14 Detroit Free Press May 11, 1924.

15 Davidson, p. 85.

16 New York Tribune, January 23, 1915.

17 Davidson, p. 175, op. cit. State of Michigan Supreme Court Records.

18 Ibid., p. 176.

19 Ibid., p. 187, op. cit. Detroit Free Press August 4, 1946.

20 Lyons, p. 266.

BIBLIOGRAPHY

Byrnes, Thomas F., Professional Criminals of America, Cassell & Co., New York, 1886.

casebook.org, a website which provides an extensive newspaper archive, classic articles about the Whitechapel murders, and intelligent commentary from participating "Ripperologists."

Davidson, Shayne, Queen of the Burglars: The Scandalous Life of Sophie Lyons, Exposit Books, Jefferson, NC, 2020.

Estate of Francis Tumblety, Probate Proceedings, City of St. Louis Archives.

Evans, Stewart P. and Gainey, Paul, The Lodger: The Arrest and Escape of Jack the Ripper, Century Books (Penguin), London, 1995.

Hawley, Michael L. Jack the Ripper Suspect Dr. Francis Tumblety, Sunbury Press, Mechanicsburg, PA, 2018.

Lyons, Sophie, Why Crime Does Not Pay, J. S. Ogilvie Publishing Co., New York, 1913.

Riordan, Timothy B., Prince of Quacks: The Notorious Life of Dr. Francis Tumblety, Charlatan and Jack the Ripper Suspect, McFarland & Co., Jefferson, NC, 2009.

Rubenhold, Haillie, The Five, Houghton Mifflin Harcourt, Boston & New York, 2019.

Storey, Neil. R., The Dracula Secrets, The History Press, Stroud, Gloucestershire, 2012.

Tumblety, Francis, A Sketch of the Life of Dr. Francis Tumblety, etc., Brooklyn Eagle Book & Job Printing Dept., Brooklyn, New York, 1893.